The Dakini Codex

NICOLE CASWELL-KERRIGAN

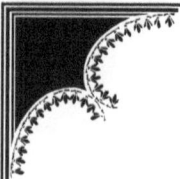
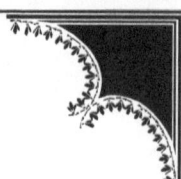

Copyright © 2025 Nicole Caswell-Kerrigan.

All rights reserved. No part of this book may be reproduced, stored, or transmitted by any means—whether auditory, graphic, mechanical, or electronic—without written permission of both publisher and author, except in the case of brief excerpts used in critical articles and reviews. Unauthorized reproduction of any part of this work is illegal and is punishable by law.

ISBN: 979-8-89419-800-2 (sc)
ISBN: 979-8-89419-801-9 (hc)
ISBN: 979-8-89419-802-6 (e)

The views expressed in this work are solely those of the author and do not necessarily reflect the views of the publisher, and the publisher hereby disclaims any responsibility for them. For more information, visit www.shholistic.com.

One Galleria Blvd., Suite 1900, Metairie, LA 70001
(504) 702-6708

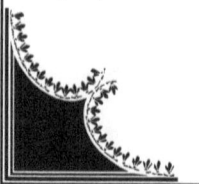

CONTENTS

The Pen is Mightier than the Sword 1
G.E.N.E.S.I.S. 2
The Shroud of Turin 3
Love Is 5
Awakening Prayer 6
Je t'aime 7
Unspoken Words 8
On Your Tenth Wedding Anniversary 9
Rose 10
To Be Young 11
My Love 12
Soul Shine 13
Twin Flames 14
These Gifts of Love 16
Tantra 17
To Those Without Pity 18
I Know 19
Feelings 20
This Heart of Mine 21
Inside of Me 22
To Travel the Road Less Taken 23
A Victory of Cost 24
Joe the Bartender 25
Gas Lighting Fires 27
The Sounds of Silence 29
Choice 30
Just Words 32
Through the Two-Way Mirror 33

Love and Pain	34
Thoughtful Prayers	35
A Moment of Clarity	36
Self-Healing	37
Whenever I Think of You	38
The Epic Saga of Christa and Nicole	39
Who Do You Think I Am?	41
The Illusion of Life	43
Listen	44
Go Further	45
Transcendental Meditation	46
Krystal Cities	47
To Wake the Sleeping Dragon	48
Soothsayer	49
Ouroboros	50
Desecration	51
The Ride	52
My Own Personal Armageddon	53
A Stitch in Time	54
In Times of Transmutation	55
The Phoenix Fire	57
Zeus	58
Apollo	59
Persephone	60
Infiltration	61
On the Cast of Seven	63
The Unforgivable Sin	65
The Holy Spirit	67
I AM FROM	69
The I AM Presence	70
The Path to Enlightenment	71
The Enlightened Mind	72

The Gateless Gate	73
Fifth Dimensional Consciousness	74
The Widow's Mite	75
It Feels Like Rain	76
Martyr	77
Bubbles	79
Good Vibrations	80
Serenity	81
Floating	82
Sensible	83
Art Is	84
Waterfalls	85
To Ethan West	86
The Beauty of Buzzards Bay	87
Nantucket Winds	88
Omniscient Onset Bay	89
Never Ending Affections	90
Give Me Wings And I Shall Be Free	91
Through Another Man's Eyes	92
In Silence I Wait	93
Emptiness	94
Pandora's Box	95
False Light Workers	96
Bon Fire	97
What I Want	98
Discovering You	99
Gifts of Golden Ribbon and Scarlet Cloth	100
Eternity	101
The Ying & Yang	102
Desire	103
A Poet, The Poet	104
Love Is	105

The Keep	106
You	107
Let Me Count the Ways	108
Arguments & Agreements	109
A Break of Light	110
The Coming of Spring	111
Gratitude	112
The Secret Door	113
Old Man Winter	114
Stargate of Aramentena	115
Spiritual Narcissism	117
Two Suns	118
Yaldeboath	121
The Cycles Keep	122
Through the Looking Glass	123
Third Eye Sight	125
The Hunt of the Unicorn	127
The Emerald Covenant	128
Transcendental Meditation	130
Crystalline DNA	131
Eyes of a Child	133
Who Do You Think I Am?	134
The Voyage of the Dawn Treader	136
Money Magic Systems	138
Gateway	139
Star of David	141
A Genuine Heart	143
To Save Face	144
Color Wheel	146
Maritime Gateways	147
Flame Holder	149
Shakti's Garden	150

Xcalibur	151
Go Further	153
Stonehenge	154
Archon End	155
The Fellowship of the Ring	157
Different Attitudes & Viewpoints	159
The Dawn of Pearl Harbor	160
Golden Rays	161
Love Phi	162
Atlantis Loop	163
Merchant Ships	165
The Fallen Flower of Life	167
Starborn Counsel	169
Plasma Particles	170
The Nibirian Grid	171
The Palace of Alhambra	172
Interlay	173
Letting Go	174
False Profits	176
The Kristic Spiral	178
The Age of Aquarius	179
Somatic Sound Circle	180
Tuatha De Rune	181
Peace Treaty	182
Expansion	183
Boots On The Ground	184
Life Elixir	186
Winged Alchemy	187
Butterflies	188
The Elysian Fields	189
Tataria	190
Copy Cats	192

The Pen is Mightier than the Sword

The pen is mightier than the sword
Through written word, laws were born
And through the word spoken above
A record of divine love.

The pen is mightier than the sword
Words cast spells when sworn
And through the grammar and syntax given
The inversions upright from heaven
Set the laws in stone.

The pen is mightier than the sword
Upon the removal, a throne was born
Camelot reigned
Its place ordained
From the removal of the sword from stone.

And so it's promised in Divine Law
The sword would be cast into the plow
And from the harvest all will bow
The pen is mightier than the sword.

G.E.N.E.S.I.S.

G is for Genesis, marking the beginning of time.
E encompasses everything, and everything will be fine.
N is for nothing when everything is found.
I is for intrinsically intuitive, and in it you will ground.
S is for spiritual. You have it in spades.
I is for intelligent, for the wisdom you gave.
S is for special. There is no one like you!

Genesis, I am so glad the world has found you!
You pray with the faith of exercised saints.
You overcame obstacles and made it in God's way.
There was never a person who had a bigger heart.
The lives you touch are golden and to them you will impart
A new and improved way of looking at life.
You will make the hearts of others blossom
with your faith made alive.
An angel that graced us will be called
Genesis, this beginning, whose heart knew it all.

The Shroud of Turin

Yeshua Hamashiach came
The ark of the covenant reign
The Shroud of Turin maimed
The living bloodstain.
And many in their demise
Cast lots over the Turin shrine
And covered over the life benign
And claimed it for their own line.
The Holy Grail toasted the cup
Was it O negative boiling up?
To keep the controllers stationed topped
Upon the golden throne did bind.
Little did they know, the rose
That set the flowering growth of glow
And so that was humbled deep below
The AB negative in mine.
And so the stories made of old
Transmute the mourning that cast the gold
And with a mark of Cain be told
All that came in time.
I carried both in this vessel
The sorcerer's stone of alchemical lessons
Transmute the sphere of Amenti tresses
From shining red to heart green rolled
For the sake of earth's ascension
Source code fail-safe and all its measures

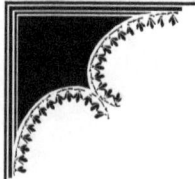
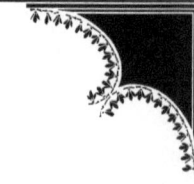

A golden portal link of treasures
Between the braided threefold cord
With living waters I set up to bind
The fractured sections of the realm in time
Sacred geometry's eternal life find
Blossoms in the center of thine
Inside it I hold the keys of heaven
And set it away from the cast of seven
Return it now like the bread causes leaven
To allow its best to rise.
And so it is in the I Am presence
My gift to mankind to know its resonance
And live the wholly of holy's presents
To know the love that births existence
In this sacred heart of mine.

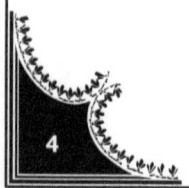
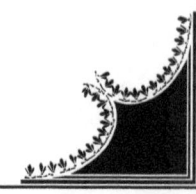

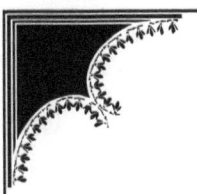
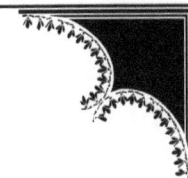

Love Is

Love is true-hearted and unselfishly kind
And bears the circumstances of trying times.
Love believes all things with hope so strong.
Love never fails and can never go wrong.
Love is faith, the epitome of God,
And through love's reflection, our self-interests are shod.
Love is forgiving and rejoices with good,
Love is believing that circumstances could
Change with time when love is mine
True love is there for you.
For love, it gives, refines, and sieves.
All the past we leave behind
All the pain that is in our minds
Love is infinite through time.

Awakening Prayer

The morning mist envelops me
And encompasses a prismed light.
The sun grounds and surrounds me
As my soul is taken to a different height.
I hear the whispers of Mother Earth.
Her maternal instincts call
Under the watchful eye
Of Father Sky
I'm surrounded by it all.
The gentle breath of rolling fog
The birds that awaken with a song
A frozen moment may not last that long
But inside me is preserved alive.

I raise my hands to the Father Sky,
And ask for strength under his watchful eye
That even if my life should go awry,
I'll be safe inside His arms.

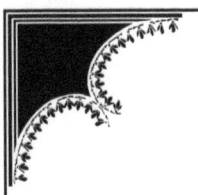
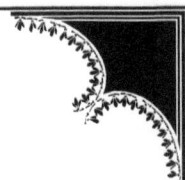

Je t'aime

Your love is the feeling of becoming one with heaven.
It is to touch the clouds and know freedom at last.
It is the starlight sky brought down to earth
to play inside the forest canopy.
It is the echo of a breathtaking cathedral.
The pristine shine of a thousand icicles.
It is addicting as sweet wine, and as lips that long to be kissed.
And if love cannot bring us these presents,
just as I give these gifts to you,
It will feel like a sting that dwells deep inside this heart
Until the tears fall down my cheeks like passionate rivers.

For I have known in my mind and felt in my heart
that it is your love I shall thirst for.
And it is your love I shall need to survive.

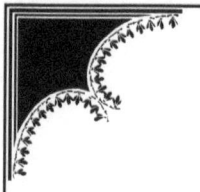
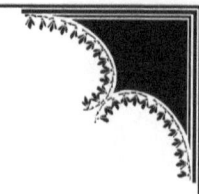

Unspoken Words

They say the eyes are a window to the soul.
I was just gazing into these lipid pools
And with this hand you've given me.
You gaze with a different sight.
This love offer that surrounds me
As these unspoken words take flight.

I trace your face with my hands
As if to remember your gaze.
Like it would be etched in my mind
On a carved granite interface.

I feel your love from the aura of your heart.
That magnificent grove that never seeks to part.
This gentle embrace in breath of sighs
Places me on a lover's high.
The sincerity of your gaze encased in tears
Holds the promise of a million years.
These unspoken words that lie unfurled
Speak louder than one may say.
In stillness it is held with time
And never washes away.

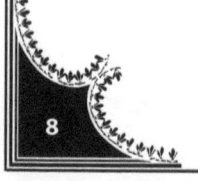
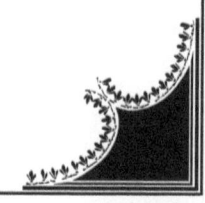

On Your Tenth Wedding Anniversary

Love is a crown of royalty
In the sheer essence of its loyalty,
Endowed upon its regal glow
In the dreams of love here below—
A collage of beautiful memories.
When true love grows,
It infinitely shows
In all its miraculous ways,
For it becomes so young
Never leaves unsung
It's love for all its days.
With the passage of time,
It embellishes like wine
And becomes more refined
Like a blossoming rose.
For love never fades
Never counts all its days,
And time becomes all of its own.

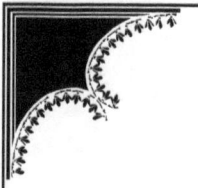
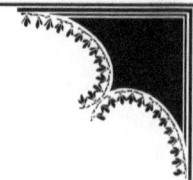

Rose

A lover's blush
A bouquet of blooms
A summer's rush
Of pink hues.
A flavor that mingles
In long-legged strains.
The cork's aroma that wrinkles
The nose of great gain.
It warms the cheeks
Like it warms the heart.
A gift to you my love,
Cheers to a great start!

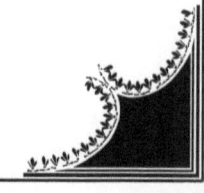

To Be Young

To see the world through the eyes of a child.
To dance on clouds all whispered and wild.
To derive a thousand words from one single picture.
And to see mankind as a colorful mixture.
To realize your dreams are all within reach.
To experience life, to learn, and to teach.
To give nothing a reason for me to grow bitter
Or lose its luster color and wither.

For this is what it means for me to be young
To never let hopes and dreams go unsung
And so after all is said and is done
I will have known what it meant for me to be young.

To see moonlight dance from wave to shore
To be content with life and not ask for more.
To find solace and pleasure in the first fallen snow
And to find joy and fulfillment in watching things grow.
For this is what it means for me to be young
To never let love and life go unsung,
And so after all is said and is done,
I will have known what it meant for me to be young.

My Love

My love is an abyss that is overwhelmingly deep
Love could get lost in it.
My love is an aged liquor
That embellishes and intoxicates.
My love is intense.
So much love I could give until you have drunken your fill,
you could no longer stand it.

My love is a ripe flower—fragile and ready.
My love is towering, as infinite as a starlight sky.
Yet my love is critical. My love could grow
in minutes, die in minutes.
All I have known is exquisite pain.
Pain near death but not entirely disillusioned.
Pain in which no poet nor judge could justify.

My love is secretive, intimate.
My love can replace pain with hopes.
My love can be spiritual, healing everything.
My love is intense.

Everything I have to give is in my power to love.
It is theatrical, dramatic, poetic, and romantic.
My love is your love, and your love is mine.
And it is no less than everything to you, to me. Always.

Soul Shine

With the brilliance of a thousand stars
And galaxies that collide in the warmth of your eyes,
I see the universe in you that creates my awareness
A mirror reflection of worlds that crashed into mine.
Whole kingdoms and ages of time
Enter into the inner sanctum of my heart.
And through these words need not depart,
I see your soul shine.

My brother and sister who have joined me in this journey,
Living on earth to change our past
And bring forth our future that is meant to last.

I must step out from my long-lost rest
To know my higher self at best
And align myself with growth of learning
In order to see my soul shine.

May all be revealed in divine time,
These twists and turns,
Victories and burns.
These tears and sorrows we grind.
I transmute and bend
And practice over again
In order to see our souls shine.

Twin Flames

My twin flame
The soul's same
Call my name
To you I came
A mirror image
I saw myself
In your rummage
Reached out to help
On the line of scrimmage
My heart melts
Set on fire
My soul ascends
My passion lit
My lover friend
Our connection birthed
On a plane
Reset by distance
It's all the same
I feel your presence
Your fire rages
Burn into reverence
The Goddess flame
I scream your name
My body melts
I drift to sleep
The dreams of you
My heart songs keep

Until the day
You come my way
And in me play
To come what may
The lover's game
I call your name
Just like a prayer
And with this beat
And know no repeat
This attraction is like a soothsayer.

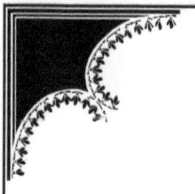
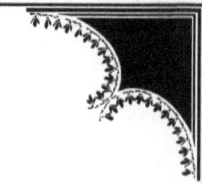

These Gifts of Love

These tokens of love
The full moon and shining sun
Starlight to hang upon my veil
To encompass and surround me
Light shining all around me
In cosmic force, these things sound
Its creation and its breaking ground
From source code, it measures grand and loud
These token gifts of love.
In my hand on finger lies
A diamond crystal to catch the eye
A token gift caught up on high
To adorn my lover's heart.
And on my bed red petals lie
Fill the air with a gentle sigh
I lay my head down on this bed
To my lover's room I am wed.
This embrace that encompasses the soul
Wrapped in angel wings of feather touch
I breathe slowly as I go
These token gifts of true love.

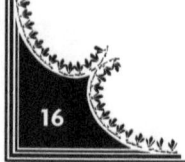
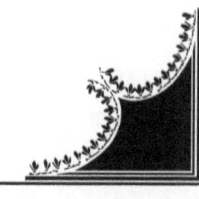

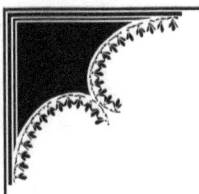
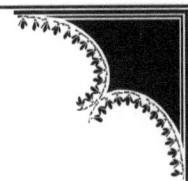

Tantra

Weaving through this moment of time,
Your timelines crash into mine.
They emerge a new beginning
In tantric line of ebb and flow.
My life exodus through you.
And in this energy that encompasses all that may be
I feel you move inside of me
As if our physical bodies collided.
Like a supernova in the sky,
I abide in the starry night,
And my soul is emerged as one.
Our lives create to have begun.
All this that lived in heart, mind, and soul.
And so it is with every newborn goal.
The thought of you conceived with cosmic force.
Creates the universe of our very existence.
We become one.
And so it is, and so it is.
Beloved I am, and so it is.

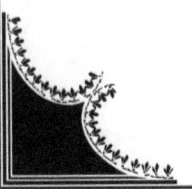

To Those Without Pity

"Cruel of heart, lay down my song
Your reading eyes have done me wrong..."
For you were told by many that I did not care.
Ceaseless love now desensitized there.
Without a word, I see you pass.
Your mind erect, your eyes as glass.
Not a single tear or phrase for me?
So was it time that set you free?
A dreamless boy so filled with passion
Left my throat still dry and my love still questioned.
The needs of love in anguish past
Made me think this love would last.
A death of heart, a bloody rose,
Withers as the summer goes
So love will always fade.
But with strength renewed and dreams renewed,
I'll wait for you this day.

I Know

I know what you wanted to say is going to please me.
I know what you might do that will make me cry.
I know what will happen in the near future,
But I am also afraid to ask why.
This hope tears at my heart strings
For this long-awaited dream.
For all my childhood memories are now foreshadowed and gleamed
I know what you want to relate lies deep within your soul
And tears from within you to reach this very goal.
The words are yearning at the tip of your tongue
And at the same time destroyed you and stung.
I know you'll cross every ocean.
You'll find your way through the storm
To find the peace of mind from your pain
And relief of the weight you've born.

I'm with you in the ocean.
I'm fighting my way through the storm.
I'm crossing my pain to relieve the weight I've born.
I love you for your struggling fight,
I'll accept you for your painful plight.
I'll show you new horizons,
The wonderful things you have to gain.
I'll turn all that is insane sane.
I'll turn all those prison walls
That leave you cold and gray
And fill it with the words you long for me to say
I'll make a temple with all your art
And fill it with gold, silver, and stars.
I'll teach you the essence of my soul
In every form, way, sound, and goal.
There is so much that this love can do
It knows no bounds for nourishing you.

Feelings

Depression roams like a drifting tide
Happiness will lack and a smile will hide
A tearing inside of flesh and of soul
A feeling of failure to a particular goal.

Pride, however, on the other hand
Tries to be held yet blows like sand
Pride may be uplifting to many of those
But leads to a failure of a particular mode.

A giving expression is not like depression
It has nothing to do with pride
A smile will grin as a friendship begins
When a giving expression cannot hide.

This Heart of Mine

Shattered and tattered and ragged for wear.
Busted and battered, burned and bare.
Tired yet wired and restless in cares.
Broken of tokens in heart and wares.
I see you, I feel you, I hurt as you do.
I need you, the real you, and the worst that you knew.
It hurt me, it swerved me, it made me stew.
It revived me, it enlivened me
This heart of mine and from that I knew.

In this moment of time
My heart was not mine
It began to chime
For it had been true.

Inside of Me

Within the quiet of my monkey mind
The chatter in my brain
The constant talk and egoic balk
That makes me feel insane
Within the spaciousness that exist
Its birthing place that now persists
To destroy the voice that resists
Within this moment of time.

Cycling along the breath work
Where the soul is closed and scared
I open my lungs to take in the air
This practiced intent to calm the fear
Among this creative year
So that with vision I may steer
My shadow self that creeps and lurks
And so with integration works
An acceptance of all murk left behind
So that in conscious forms I find
A peace within my soul mind
A transition in knowing that all things change
And suffering that feels so strange
Tries and tears to sort out all this pain
Can transmute the growth of range.
As each group cycles closer than last
In spirals of pain body's past
I grow stronger with every weighted mask
And so it is with every task
To destroy the suffering of my soul.

— Nicole Caswell-Kerrigan —

To Travel the Road Less Taken

I walk the path less traveled,
Full of brimstone and ash
And have seen my share of trials battled,
Feeling like edges of shattered glass.
I've traveled the road less taken,
Then others have not dared to walk
Or others even care to hear of
When people care to talk.

I've journeyed the road less used
That many have come to neglect,
Although the truth of the matter is,
It is not so easy to forget.

The path of the road less taken
Others have taken too,
And many have experienced that road
Of the battered and the bruised.
It may seem like you are alone
When it is you against the world.
When no one cares to know about
The footsteps you have tread
And to make all come alive,
That which once was dead
To walk the road less traveled.

A Victory of Cost

To search for you intently and know just how you feel,
As tears well in this aching heart, questioning what is real.
So I follow in your footsteps of times that we have lost
And wonder if I will see you
A victory of cost!

As I build myself a fantasy
Of loves that I have lost.
Again I ponder victory
But only that of cost.

For the love I hold so dearly
Is held with all my heart
And dangles with the string
Of a never-ending part.
My love for you is the ocean,
Which crashes in the storm
And carries your affection
I thought that you had born.
These precious memories are all that I possess,
Given me through time in an excruciating test.
So, a victory of cost loving can sometimes be,
A questioning of time and a wonderment of me!

Joe the Bartender

Joe, the bartender with a pirate's eye patch and a tasseled tall tail
And a bartender's visor that glistens a green veil
His signature drink, Southern Comforts, at best
From the deep South Carolina from Camden's great rest
He started his days as a lonely little pup
Tied to the tree of a yawning live oak
And so it began, the days of this bloke
His sentinel guard looks on with a toke
And says to the girl who showed up at the shop
"We don't sell the pup here," and that was all that she got
So she left that day with a twinkle in her eye
"I'll break him out of the clink the next time I stop by"
Known from her friends as Squeaky, she rode
To take the young pup from the place he was stowed
In the rear of the car and brought swiftly he rode
Through the back routes to a horse show he towed
And found a New England lady to finally unload
And make his place in his new Keswick home.

Step up to the bar, what's your story you brought
Are you a rescue from the life you have sought?
Do you have the blues while you drink your last draught?
What blew you in to the tie in the tree?
What caused your pirate's patch and the things you did see?
Does it change the way now you are looking at me?
The tap-danced great caper to finally be free?

I tell my tale as I hand you a drink
The spirits set sail, and the sadness did sink
I am Joe the bartender, as sly as a mink
And I give you a wave and send you a wink
Be the hero to gauge your great story and think
You can be a rescue from the lonely old clink
And set yourself free as you step up to the brink
I set myself free and I give you this link.

Gas Lighting Fires

This byzantine maze of smoke and mirrors,
Mists of haze and alabaster quivers
Shoot from directions that boggle the mind.
I tread in dark water, but in the light, I find
This battle is not mine.

Within grounding I am centered,
I see you with pitied sight.
I shield myself from painful words
In an aura of white light.

I release this twitching eye
And pain in my lower back.
This disease you spread on high
With your verbal attack.

I acknowledged what I could change,
But still it was not enough.
To see you manipulate your rage
In what you think is love roughed up.
The compliment the soul
And punch it as you go
And think this is where passion is lit
Leaves me crying over what you did.

It dims your sacred light.
How sad that within you finds
Judgment in dual mind.

In this you fight your own room of smoke and mirrors.
In my knowing, I am bestowed
That whatever said is also felt within.
While your finger points with sharp words
Three steal your heart with swords.
I would like to reassure you that my kindness is not an act.
But this final curtain is lowered, and there is no turning back.
These gas lighting fires I extinguish in love.
I pray every day for this to retire.
These diseased words and gas lighting fires.

The Sounds of Silence

When an answer is made
That doesn't reflect the heart it gave
When an explanation said
Feels the weighted heart of dread.
I seek the sounds of silence.

In the knowing deep within
The answers given inside I send
Each response that I may say
Doesn't carve to find a way
In the bridge that seeks forming
Crumbles with the sounds that are storming.
I find myself in the sounds of silence.

And so the path spirals inside
Because the answer always hides
In this knowing, I abide
And in these answers that I find
Reveal the answers that I seek
And matches the desire that is meek
Calms the storm that does abide
In these answers deep inside.
I hear the sounds of silence.

And so I begin to let go
Of all that doesn't allow the flow
And in these echoes deep below
The wells of laughter and talk bestow
The sounds of silence.

Choice

A choice that was taken
Created a forsaken
Measure of increments
That destroy the home
In overlooking right path
With no middle way
No medium of virtue
Was able to stay
And now the crack made
In quantum energy gave
A split in time
Where severance creates
A falling away
With vortex spirals
Line in rhymes
Of energy rivals
And now began
A letting go of trials
A severance of ego
In trisula strikings
In quantum creation
Of Dakini measures
In a light language tongues
Of portal treasures
Now strikes the dance
Its viral measures
On top of the cosmos
In radiant spaces
I am the enigma
The stipulation of stigma

The destroyer of dogma
And the wheel of karma
While in the wheel of dharma
The turns with life
And anti-life matters
That brought in strife
The choices were marked
Created by heart
And the quantum universe
Now traverses
The parallel lines
That crosses through times
And brings in the rays
Across solar rhymes

It's calling, it's calling
The flash for the balling
The light all enthralling
Is coming in time
From choices from choices
The heart gives the voices
The Lotus-born Master
Then comes to rise.

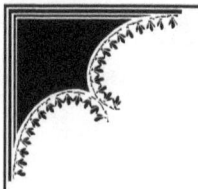

Just Words

When words that are said are not followed by action
When intent of heart is not given pure traction
When faces come and go like blurs in the wind
And no meaning is given to the spirits they send
It is just mere words spoken
No meaning, no token
No real genuine measure
Of golden heart treasure

No life force where words only fail
To concepts and dreams that are forced down to hail
When integrity and dignity do not have a meaning
Because lackluster qualities come in streaming
When no consistency is given, and frustration runs high
Because words that are spoken are not acted as nigh
And allowance for mediocrity begins
Is a destroyer of morals and an unforgivable sin
When mandates mask the spirit of God
Despite being peaceable, no respect is shod
A fading away of presence will be
The estate left desolate for all to see
A home without life is a dead place to me
Without heart, without words tread dead actions to me.

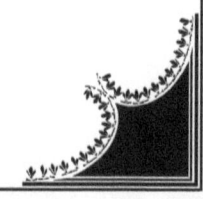

Through the Two-Way Mirror

Through the two-way mirror
I see myself
Separated as a human and the awareness mind
I envision the recollection
And its reflection
Of the current in the now moment of time
The experiences given
For them, I was driven
Down into illusion of smoke and mirrors
To scry with the mind's eye
A web of dreams sending shivers
To awaken the oneness inside
I had to die
To allow more to awaken
Allow the old to be shaken
Like an emerging butterfly
I had to let go and the fear of being so
To allow the consciousness to rise
Many questions were given
To the birthing human riveted
By the transformation made inside
Through the two-way mirror
Sent a split in time
An awakening dream
To the death of the mind
I began to step into the transformation
Knowing light is information
I am all of it in deliberation
To discover the wholeness
I find I make peace with the darkness
In oneness is neutralized
I am the light in the wilderness
And the veil of darkness behind.

Love and Pain

Take your love and make it last
Take your pain and destroy the past
You can do it if you try
So you will not die
And then, true victory will be yours!

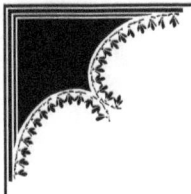
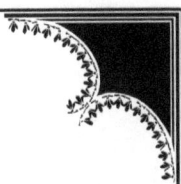

Thoughtful Prayers

I could never find an answer
That was ever left untouched.
And through my prayers an answer
That ever meant so much.
Although we are not together,
I stand my very ground
That I had a true solution to the answers I found.

Thoughtful prayers are answers that are the best that they can be,
And although a painful answer, I will gladly let you free.

So I look toward the future with pages left unread,
And surprises still surprise better left unsaid.
So when my knight in armor
Comes around the bend,
I will know my questions are answered and
my dreams are on the mend.
In my heart I will be happy, and with joyful tears I'll cry.
That I never loved another, and this love won't let me by.

Thoughtful prayers are answers that are the best that they can be,
And although a painful answer, I will gladly let you free.

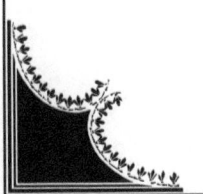

A Moment of Clarity

I see things that are so much brighter,
So much brighter than the midday sun.
I see things that can happen
And cannot be unsung.
I see a new tomorrow,
The wonderful things life has to gain.
I anticipate the moment,
The day of no pain,
For who are we to realize
That this is all a dream anyway.
That pain and pleasure is finalized
In our thoughts that hold us sway.
And with this power of knowing
Our manifestations take place
From the realms of creation
Our dreams interface.
If we dream of a world
That exists in peace
We will have found our goal
And our greatest release
This moment of clarity
I abide for my own.
I shine like the sun
That beams out and roams.

Self-Healing

Facing aft to the bedside
As light diffuses through the window pane
I witness a healing of innate knowing
That cycles clockwise and circles again.

The music streams through the air.
Its vibration heals as it turns
The crown chakra of the physical mind.
As it breaths and burns
Through the injury and disease,
The mind, body, and spirit heal
In this sliver of time,
In this moment of realization
In the violet flame of transformation.

Whenever I Think of You

If there ever was a hillside
With a blanket of grass for me head
As I dreamingly gazed at the skyscape
To see clouds dance by my bed.
If ever there was a gentle breeze
And upon me soft petals fell
Underneath the blissful spring trees
Wishing me ever so well.
If ever there was a garden
Of privet hedgerow and rose
Of lavender, sage, and rosemary
Where sunshine floods and flows.
There I would think of you often
And wish you were by my side
To laugh along with nature's wonder
Where all the pleasantries abide.

The Epic Saga of Christa and Nicole

That baby died for us! Her blinking shoes soaked in crimson sand.
I'm a dirty nurse with loving hands.
I am violet flaming, shaman naming, darkness taming,
With this skinny little Obama witch
Who wears wild eyes and cast her cries out into the air
Beside the peddling little prick,
Sitting like a stick without a word he ticks.
As the dog barks, she wags her tail
Like he wags his tongue while lightworkers prevail
To replace judgment with unconditional love instead.
I open to heart mind, to my innate knowing
And reject the high priestess minister guru
Upon whom her altar is glowing
Cast over in dogma like a dark shadow
To suggest her knowing is stronger than I.
I vomit the thought from my old soul mind.

I am the oasis, and I do what I want!
Through experience my soul is taught.
Like the ghosts that roam the haunted mansion
I seek the truth with grounded questions.
I break the habits of a troubled life
A bad boyfriend and relative strife
Release the ties, I do or die!
I ride the wave on ethereal highs
I gain the balance and know the curve
Upon my neck that sweeps its swerve.
I look up and exercise the stiffness
Upon the roads and turns its riftness.

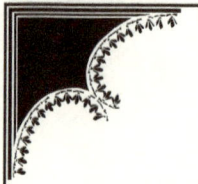
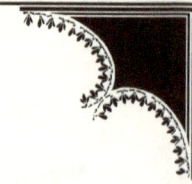

I learn to let go and try the new
Upon the darkness light then grew
I sell my soul to the goal
Like the seaweed I eat for five bucks a sheet.
I rummage the life of dreams I bought
And bring it to others on edge it's taught.
I am a survivor, a quiet contriver,
An imaginative reviver
Of coming to earth and grounding in nature's birth
I ride the wave of uncertainty,
The great unknown with a pretend lesbian friend.
I question the growth and start over again.
Exude with gladness the system of six
Of yoga walks and nutritional food
Of relationships, rest, and work exude.
I draw from these holistic wells
And upon the fairy cast my spells
I am the healer, wielder of time
And sit my home on an energy line
Between two worlds I find my time
And so I reside, and so I reside.

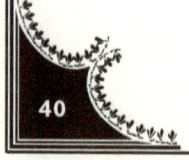
~ Nicole Caswell-Kerrigan ~
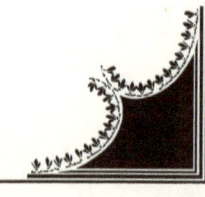

Who Do You Think I Am?

Am I like this community guitar
Hung on the wall for all to see
With an open invitation that says "Play me"?
Who do you think I am?
That I should wish for this?
A friendly embrace that lingers too long
Or the invitation of a stranger's kiss?
Do you think that I am a lost soul,
Roaming from haunted corner doors?
Do you think my love is stipend
Like all the other roaming souls
Looking for desperation
In a bottomless glass of wine?
Who do you think I am
That my light should seek to find?
The homeless cry in a tired mind.
Who do you think I am?
In this room of smoke-filled mirrors I find.
Who do you think I am?
Where does this "I am" presence reside?
I am my own woman, My own light,
My own strength,
I acknowledge my own fight!
So who do you think I am?

A thing to spite?
A thing to fight?
A thing to play a game?
A thing to hang?
A thing to bring?
A thing to sing of my fame?
Who do you think I am?

A witch to fly?
A bitch to buy?
A fling, a bird?
A quiet fuck?
A thing to suck?
Who do you think I am?

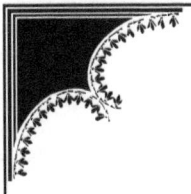

The Illusion of Life

I am tired of the labeling,
The duality conscious mind,
The chasm of hatred
On the public's time.

I am tired of hearing "Black lives matter"
As if any other color does not.
It is as if we are purposefully segregated,
And what we desire needs not to be taught.

We walk through the streets like zombies
With fluoridated pineal gland brains
Too focused on our iPhones and social media
Like a selfish runaway train.

How can we survive as a species
When we acquire more for our garbage heaps?
While hoarding material riches
While the growing rift the economy keeps?

How can we call ourself human
If we ignore our humanity?
And live in our manifest pain of consuming
Our blinding reality?

Where will the sustainability come
If we continue to sap our soul?
On the ravenous materialism
And in this venomous role?

Do we understand that we are the majority?
We are great to overturn the minority
In consciousness growing ability
That what is no longer serving the role?

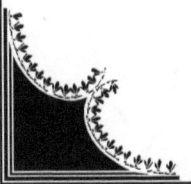

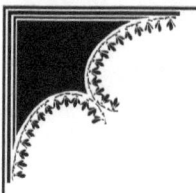 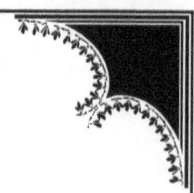

Listen

Listen closely, dear ones,
And do not close your ears.
Transmute your pain and sorrow
Into joyful tears.
Because pain is energy wasted
When it depletes the will
And your power is in your doing
And the overcoming still.

The cry of humanity,
The Crimes we all commit
Rise above it all in love,
And with forgiveness it is sent.

Create the realities that liberate the mind,
Release the chatter and from the heart you'll find,
The emptiness of space where all things expand can grow
To create a new world where we all desire to know

By experience in joy and by good health to all,
For this we were given this beckoning call
To come embodied and bring forth life
And from this heart space create in time

A measure of prosperity and ease for all
For this we listen to the beckoning call.

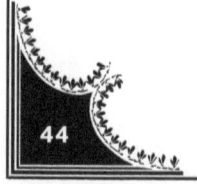 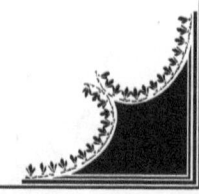

∽— Nicole Caswell-Kerrigan —∾

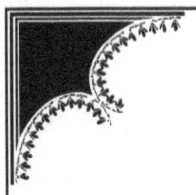
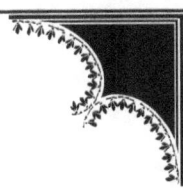

Go Further

"Go further!" you should have heard her say;
"Go further, and tell me what you find along the way."
The journey of a thousand miles begins with a single step,
So take your leap of faith through the gateless gate and always do your best.
Many trials you will find
Will have to be worked out within your mind.
But "Go further," I heard her say.
And losses too, will find you.
There are sacrifices you must pay.
Do not allow fear to deter what you do,
"Go further!" I heard her say.
For wisdom gained is wisdom earned.
You'll learn it by the day.
It will transform the essence of who you are.
But go further all the same.
One day amid the massive quaking,
You will have found that you have awakened
And the obstacles that once felt so tall
Will seem to have grown so small.
Necessity will have won the fight
Of all that has come to light.
"Go further!" I heard her say.

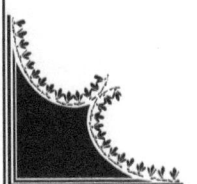

Transcendental Meditation

The ancient action of pushing past the gateless gates of the mind
To connect with the Divine and to unite humankind.
The Buddhas and the Bodisvittas from the wisdom of the ages,
The avatar of the earth though our muses and our mages.
The incarnation of our being with our third
eye of seeing.
For acceptance and compassion to help rise above
The suffering and injustice and to forgive in love.
Until we realize our nature.
The apotheosis of our minds.
Like a moth to a flame, to know
Oneness, we are the same.
Like a phoenix in the fire, we develop we grow.
We undress our desire
We reach for something higher.
And in this I do know
That our chakra crown will glow
Its rays like the corona of the sun
And so it is we are adorned, and in this beauty we run.
And so we reflect the universe we become
A mirror for all to see.

Krystal Cities

What we bring
The Elohim sings
Return to Source
From the one-eyed kings.
Peace on earth
No wars at last
The continents rise
From our founder's past
Crystal rivers lay ways
To cities below
That mark their glow
With a rainbow halo
And feed the grids
Its eternal song
Created from the Source
To go along
The triad of creators and colors combine
A number sequence and song divine
Where Kristic life may begin to shine
The I am presence between yours and mine.

To Wake the Sleeping Dragon

My voice had lain shrouded, covered in snow.
Smothered in shallow waters by the people I know.
It took great courage for this voice to grow.
And no longer totter when all was laid low.
It beats with the drum of a lion's heart.
It cries with a passion for all to start.
Listen! Listen to your heart!
You must know that it is moral and good.
Yet you've silenced it in your brotherhood.
You want complacency in what you've sought.
Found idle law over principal thought.

Your fears keep you silenced in all you brought.
Listen! Listen to your heart!
A time to speak has well arisen.
For all that lie buried, frozen, and hidden.

For cowardice and strife has set with the sun.
As the golden age arises, and now has begun.

I wake the sleeping dragon.
And shake its tale.
Melt the ice caps on its snowy veil.
Stretch the wings, and flood the lies.
Open the eyes for its time to rise!
Roar your truth, speak fire, lay waste.
Push the illusion of time to its haste.
Find the power that lies inside.
Your source code powers, it's time to ride!

Soothsayer

Speaker of rhymes
And hidden truths
Slayer of snakes
In numbers and runes
Speak your truth
Soothsayer of riddles
Uncover the lair
Of ancient sigils
Protector of portals
And creator of times
Breath fire again
In lengths of ley lines

Anchor the right
Its sovereignty turns
To awaken the dragons
And curve the CERN

No New World Order
To spite our flight
And drag us down
By the beast number rite

It's time to fly
On Source Code lines
And embody the greatness
Within the feminine divine.

Ouroboros

Ouroboros serpent line
Dances in figure eights divine
The dragon of the eternal time
Death and rebirth grant to thine
Universal heart of mine
In sequence stars and cosmic rhymes.
Great ouroboros serpent fire
Create the massive funeral pyres
And from its ashes, breaths the crier
It's life anew into it hire
Great ouroboros, seer and scryer.

Solar flares and copper wire
Coronal mass injections fry her
And when the AI is stilled
The hum of Source to so it's willed
In space dust come to all who will
Dare separate in all the hate
To become something that is sought in vain
Return to me once again.

In Akashic records, keep the ways
To never allow fallen reigns
And so, it is in final thought
What was broken now is brought
Into oneness once again
The whole of holy that thought to send
Itself in the circle of writhe
Great ouroboros, do breathe life.

Desecration

Who creates a desecration of a sacred place,
The Aboriginal home in Uluru's face?
Who creates the black magic bind to mace,
The dragon down in an underground base?
Who creates the adrenochrome extraction?
The DNA codes in animal mutations?
Who plays with the crystal citations?
And the technologies of alien creations?
Who trafficked children for sexual pleasures?
And hid their agenda in darkened measures?
Who bought out the people and their earthen treasures?
Who inverted the system in matrix sections?
I am calling out transmutations
In unlimited time span calculations.
We have issued the warning,
The hourglass is counting
The time for oneness is ever surmounting.
Understand the game and be your salvation
Or seek the destruction in liberation
To return to the Source once again
As space dust innocence my friends
It's time to return where innocence begins
And sent in love for all to win.

The Ride

I am here to perform a ride
And return to the Source all those with pride
I give back to it, the fallen stars
In gamma wave blasts from portals far
Through a thousand suns the great solar flash
I complete the Kali Yuga of times past
The executioner of Revelations wrote
The four horsemen dispatched,
And so they rode In eternity
I will look back and think
I did not compromise when we were at the brink
I did my job to create the peace
And restore the universe at least
The Luciferian rebellion could come to pass
And we would create unity that was meant to last
I AM the ascended Master, and I will not fail
No weapon formed against you shall prevail
We will be successful for one and all.

Either ride beside the Christ consciousness veil
Or serve as an enemy soon to set sail
The return to innocence is where you will go
For the alliances set with action will know
Everything is based on intention so read
The heart mind that sets this journey does plead
Its fail-safe measure that is done on high
When all was chaos is made array

Above so below, and so it is set
I match the game, and so it is met.

My Own Personal Armageddon

For all that no longer serves me,
From false support to ego and pride
To all that wields and disturbs me
And from the darkness inside
Fell from cinders and ash
Among the refineries of my mind.
My own personal armageddon
Sought to destroy all I hide

The Shiva of my soul
The ascension and goal
To wither and blacken the past.
Like tempered steel and gold
To define all I hold
And to create a future that lasts.

This is my own personal armageddon,
To bury all that has passed
And to toss the rotten fruitage of all that has come to pass.

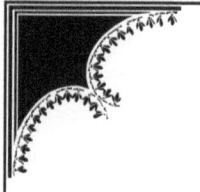

A Stitch in Time

Weaving a web of mystery
In the treasury of the tapestry
In all that life was meant to be
Exists a stitch in time.

Woven with a loving hand
In order to create all that is grand
Soul life lessons now do stand
In this stitch of time.
And so it begins on the loom
Its weft and warp that meet its doom
In this artwork of the room
Is this stitch in time.

Pictures stand so grand and tall
Tell the tales and befall it all
Frozen in the moment recall
This delicate stitch in time.
In handwork of detail combed
The mightiness of all who roamed
This masterpiece called life subjected
In this stitch in time.

Nicole Caswell-Kerrigan

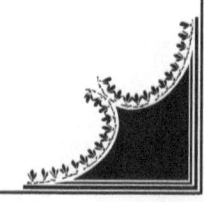

In Times of Transmutation

In the times of transmutation
When alchemy has sought its best
To bring in the blue ray beings
And return to a state of rest
When dark magic caused the hex
And marked its beast on mankind
And strained the line of humanity
Through the veins of life, they find
And the shot rang out through space
The clarion call to race
The bell that rang the pace
Through all who came to this place

Speak truth and do not hesitate
No matter the appearance may be
Those who are genuine to see
The truth that set them free
Will feel the vibration in heart
And know it dare not part
That in family lines we brought
The answer to this alchemy
Turn the attention to tide

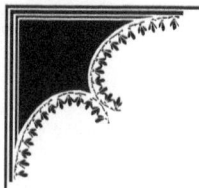
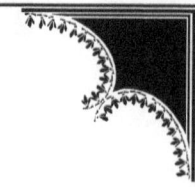

The soul family here abide
And needs to hear the call
Of the red-pill wrecking ball
In silence watch the sound
Of all who come around
To transmute this devil clown
And bring it all come crashing down
Not alone am I
I find you by my side
And family may turn the tide
But in this truth, I abide
We shore up side by side
And stronger are we who do
In strength to carry through
When tears fall down the eyes
I send your heart in mine
And turn this test of time
Through blue ray alchemy.

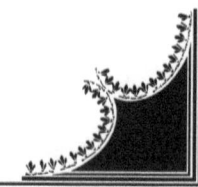

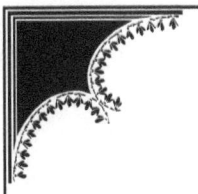
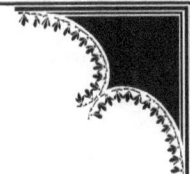

The Phoenix Fire

Into the blazing fires
The flame around me spires
As my soul it expires
To become what I inspire
I burn down and crumble
Into the ash I stumble
Until all that I am is humbled
I become one with the earth
And in its destruction birthed
The newborn soul
Like the murmur of a dragon's heart
Cast inside the plunder
A life inside it thunders
And when all hope would fail
And darkness would itself prevail
Where death itself would dare to hail
In the flicker of a flame
What expires is alive again
And beats with a wonder
The plumes rise from the ash
Rebirth and death do pass
See the phoenix's thunder!

Zeus

The clique in the clouds
Casts shadows in shrouds
And sway softly past the sky in times
Watch closely the skies
That scan earthly rhymes
And rules Jupiter's gaze
Within the labyrinth of mazes
City street ways
and mortal men's days
Watch over me father
As Thursday is born
In density scorn
The mighty oak from the acorn
To grow in these times
And become stronger in the eyes
Raised me up in the mountains
Of palatial fountains
That tell the tale
Of a youthful veil
And so, it is
Immortal and timeless
Ageless and vine less
Thy fruitage bears
And so through the yearning
Its growth kept burning
The sun sets in learning
Ascension do share
I create from the heart
To heal all and depart
My earthly walk
And so I travel home.
Back through the clouds
That cast shadows and shrouds
The spirits prevail
And to heaven set sail
It is where the silent wall wails
My heavenly home.

～ Nicole Caswell-Kerrigan ～

Apollo

The golden child of rhyme and meter.
Philosophy and bow and arrow leader.
Music and melody bequeath her.
Born aside with Artemis's twin sister
And sought refuge in the floating island.
The discus throw and laurel highlands
Sought joy in the spring bulb hyacinths
And fraught to and fro in distant wayland.

Oh, Apollo, do remember me,
Your half sister in the family tree.
No Titan clash become of me
I come in peace as of the sea

And so of Zeus who fathered us all
Beyond the veil and by the call
Came to play here one by all
Amidst this estate befall.
Among the statues great and tall,
We retell the tales and see it all.
A new story made of old
To fulfill the prophecy that told.
We moved west as to the setting sun
And so, our story has just begun.

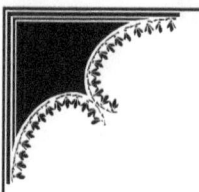
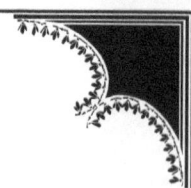

Persephone

The goddess picks flowers on a new spring day
And sheaths the wheat in her autumn play
Creating the bounty of Mother Earth's sway
And returning down under when winter gives way
She sleeps in caverns that built a palace
And resides with Hades in underground caverns
Aquifers spiral through canals and taverns
Guarded by a dog and a murder of ravens
She watches over the souls that lie below
And scatters their ashes for new life to grow
And returning to spring she casts her sow
To travel to Olympus and make it so
Creating in the clouds by her mother's watchful eyes
The seasons give way to the to the transitions gone by
And when old man winter sleeps so do I
In the quiet of the earth and in the winds of time.

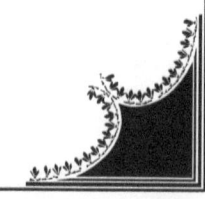

Infiltration

Pravarti is not Sati
A disciple of mine.
Reversed the incarnation,
And set it up as mine.
I did not birth Kartikeya,
The fallen angelic warrior slayer
Or created Ganesh
The obstacle destroyer.
The stories read of old
That the god mentioned above
Was scraped from the skin,
And so I am told
This is no different than
The clones created
That are made from skin cells
In labs abided.

The baths that were secret
Even Shiva could not attend
Were the Draco reptilian
Blood baths bend.

To create a beauty and fallen measure
Because the blood itself was the golden treasure.
And yet they created stealth
And trickery sent
To imitate the pure hearted
So they could ascend.
But I am back and born in time,
Set under a jubilee to give back what was mine.
My identity stolen, and it is divine.
Set up the records in universal rhymes.

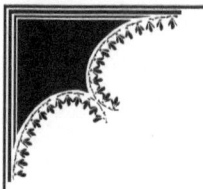

Upon my feet a mark was laid
That gave me authority when I came.
To hold a key under Christ consciousness's name
And to return to innocence those who tore the name.

I am Sati who conquered death
And resurrected into the body of breath
And whose family deep karma was sent
To right the wrongs when the name was wrent
To hurt the innocent and all that go,
But now I stand within vortex flow.

And see the light within myself.
I know the codes that break the stealth
And so, I give back the distortion flow
And return the fallen from the Source I go.
I do not request the teachings that fell
I am the master so hear the call
Understand the times, and the ride I go
As I peer into man's hearts, for this I know.
The destiny that recovers the balance
And set it right from the scornful talents.
All is to be brought to peace again
And so I ride, and so I am.

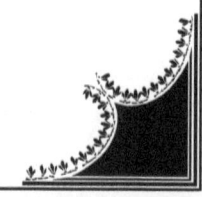

On the Cast of Seven

On the gates of heaven
I set my foundation
The dimension of seven
In royal blue vibrations
Through the remembrance
Of Ashashic sequence
In DNA codes
Of mystery school teachings
The stairway to heaven
In ascension mechanics
The spiral rises
In a universal-time matrix
By the Sirius star gate
I remember the fate
To set the dream
And ground the rate
In lullaby rhymes
The doorway of times
And spiraled within
Through cosmic rhymes
Its kingdom sits
In crystalline hue
Its walls abide
A cobalt blue
And light that shines
In heaven's divine
Sees the souls
Of halo's glow
All hearts know

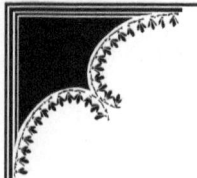

The sparkle in diamond hues
In adoration rainbows
The seventh dimension
Its celestial gates
The soul song sings
And remembers the fate
And one day awakens
The soul song vibrations
On the earthly realm
As heaven did sing
Reigning on earth
The one-eyed kings.

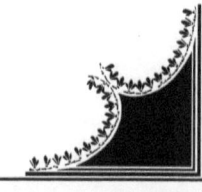

The Unforgivable Sin

To mask the breath
The breath of life
To suffocate the exhale
And bring body strife
That destroys brain cells
And causes disease
Bacterial pneumonia
And refuses the peace
Is an unforgivable sin.

Let me begin
To explain the spirit
In this action that bends
The body and mind
Through the course of time
The Holy Spirit is known as the breath of life

That animates creation and allows God through
The Holy Spirit was once ghosted who knew
Esoteric history and hidden through time
Was the Divine Feminine aspect
And is in this body of mine
To sin against spirit is an unforgivable sin.

Any mandates created that were set to begin
In any business venture takes away the free will
Of personal choice that has aspects to instill
What is best served for the person who will
Decide for themselves the health they instill

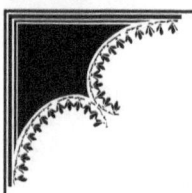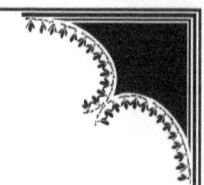

To silence the breath is yet another sin
Of freedom of speech when tyranny begins
And all who enforce this subject is sent
To eternal destruction and soul death to mend
The balance of structure that separated from the
Source To see itself as conflict and learn from resource
All Lucifer's creation I condemn on high
That creates the demon when the breath is nigh
All who invert the true meaning of the Source
And serves as a messenger to bring the remorse
Is separated out and returned to engross
Itself not knowing the destruction of course
In transmutation in spirit is what I send
To bring in the violet flame for all who resend
This decree I make known in heaven above
And above so below is sent with great love
Is my prayer to God almighty and is sent to be seen
As it measures the earth and with clairvoyance is reamed
In this decree all is bright and beamed
The great solar flash and all returned beamed
A third of itself for this is indeed
Surrendered to the Source its return is seen
In love and bliss, I reminisce
The part that is fallen I gather to me
I gather, I gather, I encompass in thee
I am presence, I am all
I am source and through this recall
Is sent in the rapture
and the rapture is seen.

— Nicole Caswell-Kerrigan —

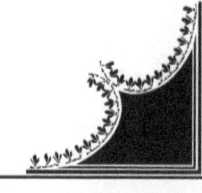

The Holy Spirit

The Holy Spirit and breath of life
Speaks wonders of creation
To let it be light
The Divine Feminine aspect of eternal right
Lies the peace within
An immortal bliss
To be this
In unity consciousness.

Despite the inversion
Seconded to diversion
Would like to surrender
The right of breath
And mask the spirit
And rest the merit
Of the Divine right to breath in life.
So they mandate a policy
Which is not law
Diversified in the man of straw
And despite the crown
Set mandates down
Covers in silence
A symbol for negligence
The mask to fit
A slavery's picture
To invert the structure
And cheat the win.
And so the battle is set to begin.

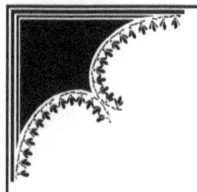
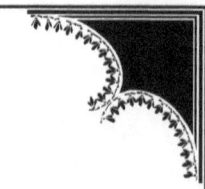

But through it all I see the light
And know the war in my own right
The common law measure
God's given treasure
My breath of life
And my own birthright.

I call in the Kristic dragons
To transmute the land and earthen treasures
And set the stars right in reversing measures
That made this structure of inverted fissures.

I AM changing the game on the eternal plane
And know this once that if you gain
You must choose the tide
And stop playing both sides
To think this strategy will cheat a win
To learn again or be sent to begin
Back to innocence of Source Code my friend.

The force is moving is stepped to diffusing
This structure of diversion
From Source is musing
And so this dance
In cosmic measures
Set the destruction of your earthen treasures
Because I know the heart
And set a mark
The dance of destruction has set apart
All the infusion that separates peace
And return it now for this to cease.

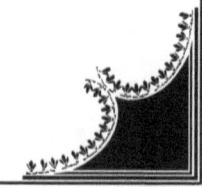

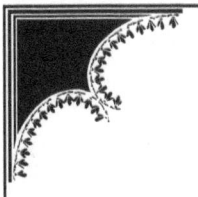
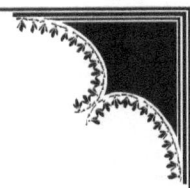

I AM FROM

I am from the Sacred I AM.
My memory was wiped in this matrix of illusion.

I am from a family of generational alcoholics.
I knew abuse in all its forms.
I am from a religious dogmatic family
And stepped away so that I knew to be
Shunned by my family tree.

I am from New England.
From Cape Cod style homes and sea faring villages.
From clam bakes and herring runs.
From ice skating on cranberry bogs
And from long walks on the jetty.

I am from a failed marriage
And years of marital neglect
I am from poverty-stricken food banks
And relationships that were wrecked.

So much of what I am has been destroyed.
Until finally I rest at nothing.

I simply am.
I've transformed and been
And created again.
And left admist
As simply I AM.

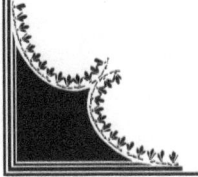
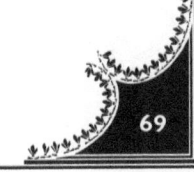

The I AM Presence

I am breathing, therefore I exist.
I am practicing gratefulness.
I am alive. I live for this moment.
Each one in its presence.
In each world alone.
The bath at the end of the day.
My hot tea and ice water.
My sound healing and shelter.
The place I am establishing a home.
I find rest in Reiki.
In crystals and music and plotted days off.
Where I can polish myself from the world made rough.
I raise my eyes into the skies
I move slowly through the matrices
From the outside energies
I breathe therefore I am
As I remember the songs of satnam.

The Path to Enlightenment

I am realizing momentous truths
Like waking from a dream
All things in life are circular
And not as they seem.
Our thoughts are our realities
Both sane and insane.
Once we awaken, we are no longer players in a game.
Yet, in order to conceptualize this life as living
We must do so all the same.
All things are circular.
There are no linear ends.
When all things come to fruition,
they start over again.
The price of truth is everything,
But, everything is not as it seems
We are no longer players in a game
When we awaken from our dreams.

The Enlightened Mind

In this unfolding of understanding
The blossoming bud of lotus life
Lifted from the mud of tribulations
Breaking through the manusha and strife.
Grows the flow of an enlightened mind.
Ascending through this moment of time.
I reach upwards for all that is divine.
And through it all, I know it is mine.
For knowledge can never be taken away.
Once its learned and anchored.
The fruit of wisdom gives way
To the ever blossoming enlightened mind
Unfurled the green leaves of peace
This untold inner beauty release
The life force that can never cease.
In this questionable waters of time.
For drops of knowledge the ocean flows.
And throughout infinity our spirit goes.
For there is of just being will ever know
Within the unfolding enlightened mind.

~ Nicole Caswell-Kerrigan ~

The Gateless Gate

There it stands before me
As colossal as the morning sun
It burns like a fire deep within me
That sears my soul to have begun.
A metamorphosis of change
As scary as it sounds
I will never be the same
Once I walk that sacred ground
I hesitate in fear.
I lift one foot in faith
So that my path may be made clear
Even though I may come to hate
All that is coming near.
Will I have what it takes
To just make it through?
This colossal gateless gate
This thing inside of you.
To push you past the obstacle
That remains so stately in the mind
To walk through the gateless gate
The things that fall behind
Are being replaced with consciousness
The zero balanced centered find
A torus field of oneness
And no separation of time
The endless eternal being
The spirit that navigates the seeing
The experience of meaning
We encompass the compassion
And step into our mission
The reason for our coming
To see clearly through the lense
The path that leads us home.

Fifth Dimensional Consciousness

We are the perfect reflection of God.
A universe in our soul.
We are the vast expanse of space
In our effortless illuminating role
We are the manifest creation of ego shod
We are the discipline of the staff and rod
Our spirit self resides with its truest interface
It is the thumbprint of everything and nothing in its trace
We are the Bodhisattva
The Buddhas and the Bodhichitta
The clear crystal illumination of sky
I am you and you are my
Reflection of evolutionary bliss
In this space we reside
In our peace, in our midst
We are the realization of God's conscious mind.
And so it is in this one moment of of mine
We are the Alpha and the Omega through both space and time.

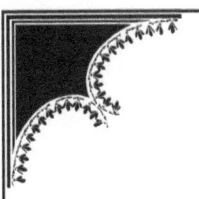
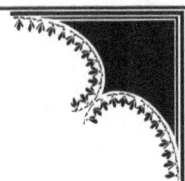

The Widow's Mite

You say you haven't much to give,
But, you give your all refined and sieved.
A pearl of high value is what you've become
Yet, all of this worth to you is unsung.
You say "I wish to treat you right
But all I have to give is this widow mite."

Truly I do say to you,
You give more than all the others do!
Meek is your presence, always ready to listen
Great are your thoughts when they are polished and glistened.

Christ-like is how you try to be
Kind to thy neighbor in loyalty.
And so these things were written above
Because you deal with other in Christ-like love.

It Feels Like Rain

I thought of how I would love you
I thought of what I would say
I thought of when I would hold you
On that fateful day.
The blues came and it feels like rain.
Would I soothe your cry?
Or would I pass you by?
The hope of now knowing you
Leaves me to question why.
The blues came and it feels like rain.
How long must I wait to meet you?
Knowing this may not be my time.
How long do heartaches linger
Until I finally call you mine?
The blues came and it feels like rain.
For my unborn child who never came.

Martyr

As I approach my home, just like a ghost I see.
There is no one to welcome me.
There are no flowers, there are no applause.
There is no parade, no praise to laud.
There is no shall to befall my neck,
A welcomed kiss or a lover's peck.
Where is my beloved people?
My village and my house?
The silence is baffling,
No family, no spouse.
I see the tree whose leaves are gone
In brittle waves stumble into the ground.
My body is drawn to lay down on
These leaves that sing my song.
These leaves are like the people whom I once knew.
That were vibrant and full of life they grew
But they withered away and fell to the ground,
And now they lie there without even a sound.
I have come back home, but where have I gone?
Brought back from the war prison without even a song.
Not far from my house, I spy with my eyes
A gravestone with my name so proudly displayed.
A martyr, a hero, a whisper of name.
There the memorial lies where my mother's heart broke
The marker of my life that is now forsook.
I hear the stories like an echo on the wind.
My mother had died from her sadness within.
My father soon followed, the grief was too much.
Death then swallowed that familiar bunch.
I cry out to God, "What has happened here?"
"That I must witness the aftermath there?"
Am I dreaming a dream, do my sight tell me the truth?
Who has taken my place in this land once so good?
I wonder myself, am I still alive?

Or an angel that walks in this moment of time?
Who are these children who now take up this space?
Who play like waves my beating heart trace?
My lover's home in ruins now lays.
Where the brittle leaves tumble and stay.
The walled fence where life once knew,
Now carries the abandon my pained heart grew.
The reality now washes over me in waves
And through this grief, sleepiness came.
I arrive at my home and fall at my knees
Like a prayer and soothsayer, I make my pleas.

Though the house lay in dust
My guitar is a must
In the corners and shadows it came
It draws me to play
Though the strings are tattered and torn
Like the strings of my heart, so worn and forlorn.
But if my heart strings should play my final song,
I shall bring it close to my chest and know no wrong.

As I play the children come to mind.
The familiar face of my long lost lover I find.
She is now my brother's wife in this moment of time.
And so with a tear, I say my goodbyes.
I play her a song and lay down my life.
I wish no ill will or to disturb the living,
I will leave on the waves the ocean I'm sending.
There is nothing left for me in my home
So on fair winds, I shall travel and roam.
Like the brittle leaf caught in the wind.
I will cast myself asunder and begin again.

~ Nicole Caswell-Kerrigan ~

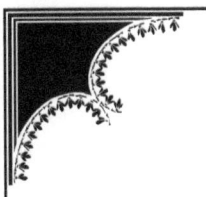
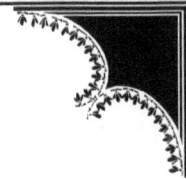

Bubbles

The baby plays with piercing blue eyes
Laughs in the light rays
Of the azure blue skies.
Spheres of soap float through the air.
Its presence permeates with a blissfulness there.
I am grateful for this.
In the manifestations of innocent joy
In the life of this child
And the heart of every girl and boy.
Who continue to create with love and play
The example shown to us this day
In a moment now swept away
We remain. We stay.

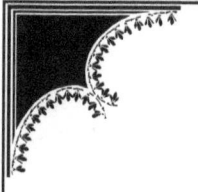
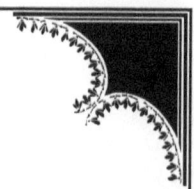

Good Vibrations

Twilight streams through the trees,
The sunset flares with golden light.
Its sound resonates with the breeze
And the fireflies burn bright.

A hungry echo vibrates
The sounds of spirits call.
The magic of the forest life,
Beyond these dimensional walls.

The drums hum with surrounding life.
And of vibrations vast.
Ancestors from our previous life.
Come with invitations of the past.

The animal totems observe,
The birds break with song.
The frogs chirp in chorus
And the crickets sing along.

The atmosphere vibrates
The energy of the earth.
As the sun is brought to bed
With a joyous mirth.

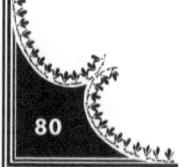
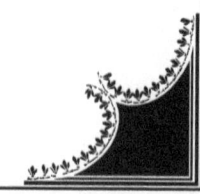

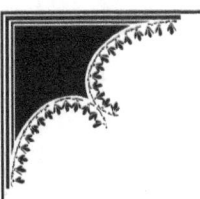
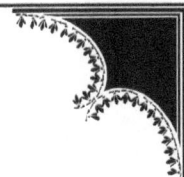

Serenity

As I lay me down to sleep
I give to you my soul to keep.

Can you find me over there?
In a peaceful place inside your stare?
Forever my love will always be there.

My heart belongs to this needed rest.
To recalibrate, then give you my best.

And when I do, I'll give you more
Than you have ever known before.

Like the crashing waves of a broken shore
Please! Do not turn your back upon the sea!
This power of love even overcomes me.
It is the glimpse of all that makes up serenity.

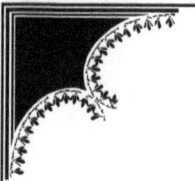

Floating

I feel lighter than the wind,
Breezy and carefree.
Something has lifted this heavy heart
Replacing the negativity
With tears of joy and serenity.
I am lifted up on high
Like the clouds in the sky
Breezy and carefree, lighter than air.
My once shadowed heart
Is shining inside of me
Radiating through every touch
I am grateful to feel so much
In this floating moment of time.

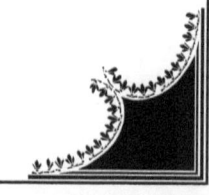

Sensible

I can hear the gentle melody of bird songs
The cars that slowly rumble by
I can feel the embrace of the sun's rays
Fall upon my shinning face.
Near my feet is the realm below
Endowed with creation's bow
Surrounded by nature
With dreams that bombard
I soak in the treasure
And in it I laud.
All this life around me
With so many things to explore
It is this peace and serenity
That I couldn't ask for more.

Art Is...

A rapsody of melodies and memories unfurled
That makes ballerinas dance and ice skaters twirl.
A field full of roses that bloom in the summer's sweetest air.
As dozens of flags wave in the neighborhood fair.
The innocent laugh of children at play
Or the time fly by stories old people say.
Whisteria painted and climbing up an old maple tree
Or whispy green foam kissing the clear blue sea.
A rapsody of melodies in a colorful collage of words
That provides the essence of creation and the motivation of the world.

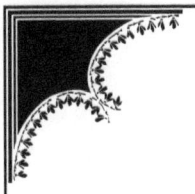
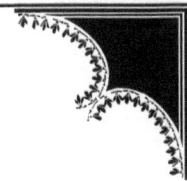

Waterfalls

In nature calls
The waterfalls
And all befalls
The sound of liquid magic
Perishes in the fabric
In sheets of white velvet.
Trailing from blackened rock
Carrying all it brought.
Of gold stone and sediment
Changing and erroding the land
Like a snake on parade
Making the oridinary grande
Pulverizing stone into sand.
In nature calls
The waterfalls
That perish in their liquid magic
In sheets of white velvet.

To Ethan West

Take my hand though fantasy land
Watch me walk you through
For the beauty that grows and everyone knows
Is the beauty inside of you.

The Beauty of Buzzards Bay

What a wonderful place the bay can be
With rolling hills that scourge the sea
Windswept clouds in a painted sky
And gulls that give their shrilly cry
To capture the essence of the bay
Is more than words could ever say
The quaintness of New England's past
Furnish it's character in its stoic cast.
Oh, how it shows it ethnic glow
Nestled in this place below
Wrapped up in its hilly cliffs
Are winding beaches and sandy drifts
Past the drifts is the ocean blue
That sparkles with a diamond hue
In the embellishment of a seasonal array
Are the inspiring landscapes of Buzzards Bay.

Nantucket Winds

The flags unfurl from the Nantucket winds
As adventures spry around every bend
Lushious green trees peek their heads
Over cottages and mast that lie overhead
The roads await this New England day
With cobblestone roads to search and to play
Every garden is an adventure
A secret enterprise
Every wind that passes
Unfolds in the sky
Unlocks the suprises that creep around bends
As a new day arises in Nantucket winds.

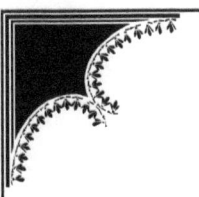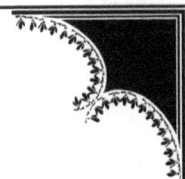

Omniscient Onset Bay

The water shines at Onset Bay,
It's inspiration is more than one can say.
What a breathtaking place for me to be
With chiseled bluffs following the curves of the sea
It's billowy winds cast in again
And send their breath upon the trees
That give their shade and stand sentinel glades
A place where boats find a safe haven wades
Tosses to a fro with each wind filled blow
And laps effortlessly on the shore
It's sandy shores casts from bends and brooks
That finds its way through cat in nine tail reeds
Each stand along and find their song amidst the breeze
Overlooking the diamond water
The village built from long ago
Peaks their heads and rooftops follow
Among the glades of evergreens stow
And so I observe a picture taken
Written in the heart unforsaken
This memory that paints its way
Unto time and flies away.

Never Ending Affections

Thoughts are exchanged in words
Words which I only dreamed could come true
The truth being made manifest
Through all you say and do

Is the truth of our reality
When thought is born into view
And spelled into words written
Enchanted to become
And so it is done
These never ending affections
Rang out and sung
Look life into direction
And steered into love.

Give Me Wings And I Shall Be Free

A beautiful bird there once was,
With the capacity to rise far above.
Beyond this world it left behind
The sky was the limit for this one to find.
A feeling of freedom radiated through
Her wings which made her dreams come true.
Unfortunately, there would come a day,
When she could not fly so far away.
The world beneath her she left behind,
Weighed down her wings, her heart, her mind.
The world beneath her caught her still,
Left her captive and hurt her will.
These wings are my power to rise above
The world that would like to steal my love.
A captive bird this heart is to me
With no time to escape and unable to feel free.
But, this glimmer of hope that lies on the horizon
Is one day soon to realize satisfaction
These wings I had I will gain again
In hope, in love, in life, my friend.
And so a new found freedom I will gain
To renew my power and my life to maintain.

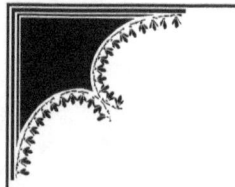

Through Another Man's Eyes

I might seem a little strange, but I believe I am misunderstood.
For my way of approaching things is not the ways others would.
Could you look through my eyes please and see the other side?
You maybe surprised by the glorious things you'll find.
Then, you would know who I really am,
The reasoning you haven't seen,
The sides that lie unbeheld.
This world of thought is not just a dream.
It maybe idealistic
It maybe a little wise.
But to me this world is realistic
If you would only look through another man's eyes.

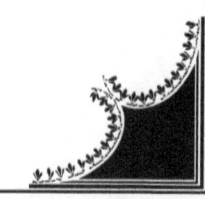

In Silence I Wait

Though it is hard to say what I am feeling,
At times, it may have me reeling.
While an explanation may sound appealing,
Is disasterous to start.
So, in quiet silence I find my mind.
Not from acceptance, but to become kind.
To the sensitivites of the heart.
And still, I wonder if there will be
True tolerance between you and me
If only you could really see
What you fear lets us be
Not together, but apart.
In silence I wait. I pray for the day
When ego will be washed away
Even though I may
Be broken at heart.
Convinced with penance it will reap
Set with guilt for conscious keep
In immersion it will seap.
Only division between us.
In irony we hope to find
Oneness in our hearts and minds.
Only lonely to be left behind
Admist all this fuss.
In silence I wait to exhale
For love, not ego to prevail
That on fair winds we do sail.
That enlightenment be our guide
For who are we if we do not abide
By humanity to guide our hearts?
And so it lead me to this query
Deep in my heart so weak and weary.

Emptiness

There is an emptiness inside of me
It feels like a lonely room
With no warmth of heart to fill and bloom
There is a barrenness to my soul
Like the echo in a cavernous hole
That returns to me the same as it came forth.
I am emptied of dreams and hopes
My life has been destroyed so well.
I wait to exhale
Putting one foot ahead of the next
And opening my mouth to feed myself.
I lay down this weary soul to rest.
The crows await to watch over my body.
As if their hungry eyes could carry me away
Their haunting cries cast shadows in the dark.
Will I simply fade into nothing?
Will the nothingness then turn itself inside out?
Is it my ego that is dying or is it my fear?
Will I live my life looking back over the rear
View mirror so I steer clear of my goal?
Is this my Master Class?
My end at last?
My exodus that passed?
To break through the mass
Of illusion and decay?
Will my sadness fade away?
Will this loneliness stay?
Why should I feel this way?
I ask as I stare into the emptiness of this room
I call myself.

Pandora's Box

Secrets that lay hidden and locked away
Kept from the eye of of open display
Evils that lay
Shrouded in a box of mystery
Carefully latched and hidden inside
Like a safe for misery
All that complied came to be
Opened in curiosity.
As a gate is released
All that came to be topped
Rolled through earth where currents flowed
Upon the dark waters mystery told
Released the misery on high
All the ghosts that came by
Reincarnated through time
To transform their works on high.

And so Pandora's Box was born
The prison planet where all was torn
Upon the tears that cry forlorn
On the planet to feel the scorn.

The IGIGI of fallen ones that lay
In soul reincarnation play
To practice an ascention and find a way
How many would hear the call?
How many of these would know their fall?
And rise again from the box
That ticks through time and released the locks.

False Light Workers

The false light worker
The fallen angelic
The leader of deceivers
In Lucifer's veil
What have you say
In the Medtronic coding
The black hole systems
That light your way?
The Fibonacci numbers
That devour its own spiral
That can't sustain Kristos patterns hold sway
The inverted matrix
And the blinded followers
That included myself in this mirrored play.

But now I see a deeper awakening.
One not held to the false ascension programs
The diagrams that show my crystalline DNA.

It's time for love to transmute the darkness
The duality in our world play
When one form splits from the other
To study itself along the way.
We fought wars convoluted
while we forgot our wholeness held away.
Return to Source as space dust, dark flower
It sets right your constant power play
We save ourselves by remembering our Kristic pattern
And the consciousness born into the day.
Return to innocence, ascension and wonder
Until the last enemy death has seen its way.

Bon Fire

The embers breathe fire
It's movement flickers with a flame
The smoke rises in the spire
And the warmth calls my name.
The clouds ascend into the heavens.
And vanishes into the sky.
The stars glitter like the embers
And like fireflies in the night.

They call me on the wind
Like a Phoenix to a flame
The smoke fills my lungs
The embers breath my name

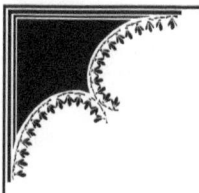

What I Want

What I want is a safe place to fall,
To be sheltered from the storm
To be loved and warmed.
To explore your horizons
To be part of this game
To know my time is alloted
And to be honored as the same.
I want my sexuality to blossom
To leave fear and let love bloom.
I need to know you may be there
When you leave the comfort of our room.
I need to know all that I am investing
Is giving you everything I am
And this is held in the light of your eyes
Through the spirit of a true gentleman.

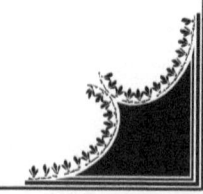

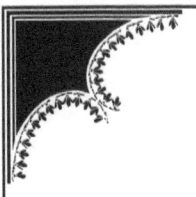
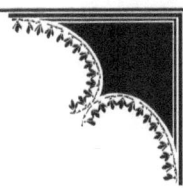

Discovering You

There is a familiarity
Like the presence of being home.
There is a heartwarming feeling
That I will never be alone.
Your gentle words fall like rain on a newly blossomed rose
This hope in life you give is more appreciated than you know.
Words fail the simple phrase, "Oh, dear. I think I love you so."
It like holding your heartbeat in your hands.
The gentle quivered drum beats onto something grande.
I see my life flash before me.
In the measure of your eyes.
Like pages in a photograph,
Between you and this heart of mine.
When I sleep at night and draw my dreams upon my bed.
I feel your energy come to me as if our arm held my weary head.
I with the the morning. The sweet thought of you on my mind.
In crowds your face is swarming, captured in this corned sight of mine.
How magical you carry me, through these thoughts in time.
And so it is, I discover you.
In every unfurled leaf, in every breath I breathe.
In this dream stage love of mine.

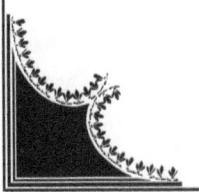

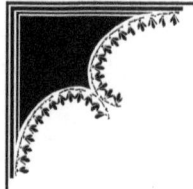
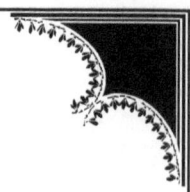

Gifts of Golden Ribbon and Scarlet Cloth

I shall love you passionately and totally.
With the grace of God's hands, be captivated by the
shimmer and fire of your eyes.
Like a window into the depth of calm waters
Your love has broken through a brilliance in my life.
In my dreams, I see you as my one true love.
Carrying alongside you the breath of silence.
Whispering in the wind like the gentle breeze of a bird's song.
You advocate your deepest affections.
Like the ancient trees of an enchanted forrest
Whose love for the glorious sun reach ever upwards and heavenbound
Your love brings me to a higher ground.
And upon it, you have rained down many wondrous gifts
Like the gentle copious showers.
And much like this fragile flower, you have chosen me from the garden of life.
I pray that every breath I take may bring onto you solace and fufillment.
All the days of my life I shall love you.
You have freely given of life's most wonderous gift
Wrapped up in golden ribbon and scarlet cloth.
For this I am thankful.
For this I am blessed.
And with this you will live eternally in my heart.

~ Nicole Caswell-Kerrigan ~

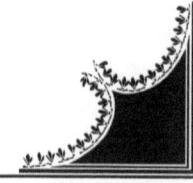

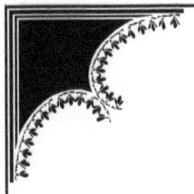

Eternity

When we confessed our love, it embraced us.
Collided two worlds now living as one
With the dawn of each new day, our love blossomed
It became brighter, deeper and more revitalized.

The night you told me how deep our love became,
Each word lifted my spirit, healed my soul and made my devotion flow.

From then on, our love was etched in stone, eternal and interchangable.
I saw myself in you and you in myself and never before did I
feel more loved.

I am so thankful I have you. You have given me,
shown me and taught me true love.
I hold you so deeply in my heart, it overwhelms me.

I need you to confide in and to explore your distant shores.

I am astonished by your celestial love.
Wonder how I ever could attain you. Never feel I deserve you.
Never fathom how such a beautiful man could love me.
I am eternally indebted to you.

You are the sparkle in my eyes, the happiness of my smile
and the love of my life.

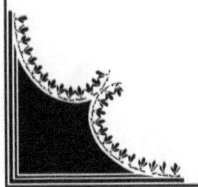

The Ying & Yang

My spirit dies
My soul cries
My tired eyes
Has seen all that I can see.

God knows I tried.
I wrench, I writhe.
I have gone inside
My own mind
For what I have yet to find.
I cannot abide.
I wish I could dream
To all that seems
Captive now freed
No more suffering.

The ying, the yang
The chaos sang
The big bang.
The good, the bad
The calm and mad
All inside of me.

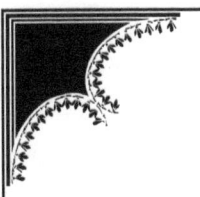
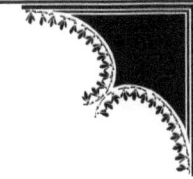

Desire

I want to see you come undone
When all your walls come crashing down
And all that is left to see
Is a wild abandon inside of yourself for me.
Encompass your fears, your hopes and dreams.
This thousand mile journey inside of you.
All this that creates you.
For this is what I know is true.
To understand, to be, to do
Your secrets, your fears, your love, your fears
Are safe inside my heart.
I will try, I will abide
To be good to you my dear.
I do not wish to harm or hurt
Or to make you feel on full alert
To know what you may feel free to desert
All that is held back from me.
And in return I give you this,
My naked soul, my heart, my bliss
And if you would try to encompass this
The world inside my soul.

A Poet, The Poet

Her heart filled with contentment, she rang out her voice,
Which fell from her lips and lie sweet and so moist.
She spoke of heartaches of so long ago
Etched in granite and carved like stone.
She spoke of reveries alive like fire!
Striking and bold and without attire.
She mentioned dreams in such a soothing tone.
That brought comfort to the sick and all those who mourn.
A celebration of words is what she became,
A poet, the poet for some painted name.
She referenced colors of a talented palette
Made from emotions that thundered and galloped.
Words that lie still, like dead graven souls
And words that stood firm like young readied fouls.
A poet, the poet for some painted name,
Of high points and memories and emotions that pained.
A poet, the poet is music in words
Celebrating life in the human world.

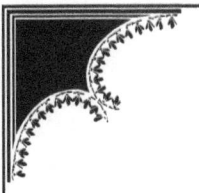
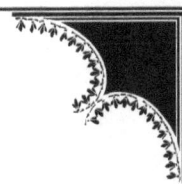

Love Is...

Love is true hearted and unselfishly kind
And bears the circumstances of trying times
Love believes all things with hope so strong.
Love never fails and can never go wrong.

Love is faith, the epitome of God
And through love's reflection, our self-interest are shod.
Love is forgiving and rejoices with good
Love is believing that circumstances could.
Change with time when love is mine
True love is there for you.
For love, it gives, refines and sieves.
All the past we leave behind
All the pain that is in our minds
Love is infinite through time.

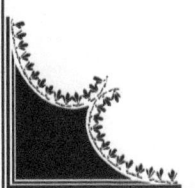

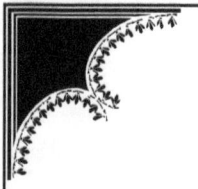

The Keep

Break down these walls of iron and ash
Blackened by fire of a tulmultous past.
Tear down these barricades of cement and stone
The ego bulwark built that retains me alone.
Create inroads of compassion and love
May ways in the maze of stone
The bizintine briar of roads
And still I know
In the crags of rocks that grow
Out from the stone
The tree of life
Break open from stife
And give forth life
You have been imprisioned too long.

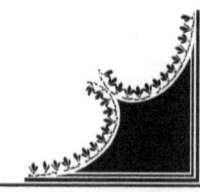

You

In my dreams, I dream of a lover.
In my heart, I love no other.
For all the spontaneous things you do
Have me constantly thinking of you
Everywhere I see your face
For every time, song and place.
In the moment that you glimpsed my world,
I never felt alone again
For all my dreams came unfurled
When I put my trust in you my friend.

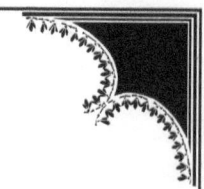

Let Me Count the Ways

How much do I adore thee?
Let me count the ways,....
As infinite as the starlight sky
Or the drops of water down a mountain creek.
How many leaves can you count on a tree?
Or how many turns exist in an infinite maze?
The story unfolds in a babbling brook.
It whispers in the breeze wild and forsook.
It creeps in the ground with Mother Earth's beat.
It sweeps in the sounds and rhythms repeat.
The intensity of breath, our God given Source.
The immensity of myths and legends foretold.
It's the shine of the sun and of a King's crown.
And beseeches the vagabond on common ground.
It's the warmth of a lover's touch, the sound of a lark.
It's everything that means so much when love is embarked.
And this is what it means when the ships mast unfurl.
It's the voyage of time in every nook and curl.
It's the gentle embrace of Heaven's Gate.
The welcoming arms lovers satiate.
It's the pros and the cons,
It's the rights and the wrongs.
It's the entirety of the Ying and Yang.
It's the Divine roles in the turn of tides,
And it's my destiny to maintain.

~ Nicole Caswell-Kerrigan ~

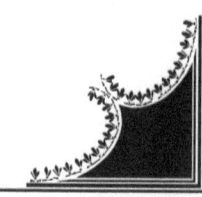

Arguments & Agreements

It's a shame to see people walk away,
With pride in their hearts and selfish dismay.
It hurts to see someone walk out of the house
Leaving behind the pain of a spouse.
Oh, how it brings a tear to my eyes,
To think such a division a family couldn't despise.
And with such joy that was shown just moments ago,
I guess there are things we will never understand or know.

A Break of Light

The heaven drapped with stars line a glistening sky
As a birds of prey wave, their wings flash by.
The trees that tower, all windblown and torn
Echo the call of a churning mourn.
The fog rolls in and listlessly plays
Amoung the waters dark and stark gaze.
The animals that play so quietly along the river
Fill the breeze with acrid shivers.
As if a spirit tried to tell
The tale of the old wishing well.
In amber fields, on moonlight nights
Under starlight skies bedazzled in white diamonds
The darkness remains a veil which covers the land
And plots to overpower with a frightening hand.
Just when the forrest fills with shadows from the moon
A feeling arises that something will happen soon
A break of light hits the firery night
With colors of a bloody rose
The sun arises, the corona is seen
As the night sleeps and goes.

The Coming of Spring

Winter's breath now fades away
As spring is in the air
The arrival of it has come today
With the hope of weather fair.

The crocuses poke their sleepy heads
Through the winter's last fallen snow.
And linger on the dainty stems
Upon the earth below.

The budding trees awaken
With prideful glory seen.
And blossom with a lacy fashion
Its fancy flowers gleamed.

Oh, happy spring! Oh, happy day!
The daffodils have come to play
The tulips laugh with earth's delight
In the coming of spring's fairsome sight.

Gratitude

Your simple acts of kindness have
Touched my heart in many ways
So much so I am speechless to give
This gratitude of many days.

I know my life is richer for
Knowing you and your galore
For all that you stand for
This gratitude in my heart.

Your example of unselfish love
This serviced life brough from above
And so I sing out with song
The jubilance in hands of spades
You've touched my heart in many ways.

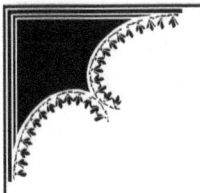
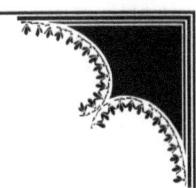

The Secret Door

A secret door, locked and untouched,
Lies in the corner of a shadowy hutch.
It has but one key which has not been used.
But, twisted and torn and fragile and bruised.

Inside the windows peer colors so bright
That glow oh so dimly in the mystical light.

If perception gave way to see all the way through
Wonderful things could happen to you!
The colors would dance with dreams and of love
That long for the time you will rise above.
That withered key that lle in your hands
To open the door that firmly stands.
Then, the colors inside would turn to you
Along with this world I built for two.

To share all my dreams of this shadowy hutch,
Would unlock the fear that imprisoned my clutch
Let my colors free and you shall find
That this love I fear will be both yours and mine.

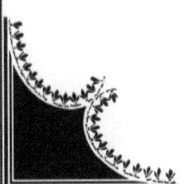

Old Man Winter

Words fell from his lips
Like featherweight snowflakes
Crystalized in the wind
And the gentle sway of grey trees.
Play upon his mountain brow
The air sank to the earth
Heavy with snow as
Winter rolls
Its windswept words
Falling from his lips
Of old man winter's world.

Stargate of Aramentena

The 12th dimensional Stargate that allowed the Big Bang of fall
Through the Isodora templates and the reverse engineering of it all
It remembered in my template the DNA structures intact
I send my love with intention to repair the explosion back
Through time that allowed the destruction
So the universe can be repaired
I send the eternal life lotus
To seal the Source Code trail
And allow the stargate structure to remain whole again
Bringing Source creation functions to begin again
The fall of Aramentena effected the Lyrans too
And falls created thereafter are to be made anew.

So as above as below
The heavens reach its field
To transmute the broken by the vecca shield

The crystals of Paladora, the wholeness of peace throughout
May make the universe spoken to effect what marks the shout
And all those under the gate lines that wish to connect to Source
Will find a lotus waiting for the unity of course
And all the fallen aspects return to me again
To remember the original love and bliss I send
Not remembering as separate as we all are one.

Like flowers in a garden, the variety we run
We contemplate our aspects in each other trace
The source is all related to each and every face
Being infinite and loving I call all to the place
By the side to work with wholeness and in all interface.

The structures will be casted in Violet fire too
And placed with rainbow prisms
The crystalline anew

It will glow and not forgotten
All is known with love
And so what is now rotten
Will rise above with song
In light and sound creation
With colors are now set
The love of bliss vibration
Makes new what is now wret
And heaven sings with glory
All aspects now reflect
The earth now send its timeline
To organic Vecca set

The golden nature of creation
In prosperity recall
The love all had received before there was a fall.

Spiritual Narcissism

Spiritual narcissism in believing a lie
Created a superiority in thinking ties
For controls in chaining the mind
To reflect a false paradigm.
Know the character that reflects in glass
The mirror image of what is passed
The lack of love and heart mind sat
Upon the projection to crush the mat.
That treads the gaslighting down
And steals the heart and sovereign crown
It despised the Law of One
And unity consciousness to work for spun
Out of control to influx grand
And reach the power to control the hand
The ugly ties that rule the land
In transmutable waves through warps and bends
Stand in truth and show your light
Know the reflection is sent in spite
And return the image with all love's might
It cannot portray a lie
And find a false paradigm.
True leadership reveals its strength
Is not afraid to see the length
In all the mastery that comes in perspective
Can find the jewel in the lotus elective.

Two Suns

Two suns in the sky
Release the binary set reel
The plasma rays
On the days
Of creation hayes
The DNA activation
Of Ascention stays

Where are we in the space time continuum?
Where is the orbit of our second sun?
Must Source create the experience
For our ascended earth to have begun?

I search the inner earth
And in vortex frequency find
The eternal life lotus beams
The inner sun that trines

I seek the pages hidden
To find the story of
The blue sun known as Nemesis
The twin flame journey won

I call back missing aspects
This broken matrix gave
To find the fixes hidden
In the fallen architecture save

What things require presence?
What things come with grace?
What things serve the consciousness
Of eternity's face?

— Nicole Caswell-Kerrigan —

The Yuga years in cycles
That destroyed the earthly plane
And fractured sections of Tiamat
To become an asteroid rain.

The violet fire reaches and golden light embrace
The features of fractured measures
To fix the mark of space

I call the OM of fire
The phoenix rebirth of hire
The flames around it spires
To create was is inspired.

I birth the concept of
The golden ring of love
To bring the blue sun god
And activate the land below

The oroburus sleeping
Must wake now in this time
The dragon gates of reaping
The land that rises find

The continent of MU is calling
The echos of the land
The sprawling land of Atlantis
To rise from the ocean again

The flip of living waters
Salt tears to sink through planes
And rise the fresh flowers
Of the desert rose through rains

I call in the divine
The triad of mine
I call in the rays
Of ascended days
To realize through the haze
The resplendent brilliant days.

And so it is with I AM
The presence set to be
The miracles set to happen
Within the avatar of me

I see.

Yaldeboath

The YHWH matrix, the jealous god
Who was created by Sofia from smoke and ash
Developed the material world in in a jealous wrath
To take for him while enshrouded in clouds
And think the name be honored in rounds
Through the Kabbalah and ancient text
A false father god that enveloped and meshed
The wars to preserve his state of mind
Sought suffering to those of whom he did bind
Entrenched in dogma not unity find
To create fear in the eyes of mankind

I entered into the world of this realm
And raised by dogma my mind overwhelmed
By powers that control by abuse and neglect
To make my soul small in darkness I felt
The Phoenix inside me now turned into ash
And thoroughly destroyed by brimstone and shame
Began to rebirth and call my soul's name
I listened in whispers as something above
Reminded me of empowerment and love
And through this call I heeded on air
To birth the existence that forms now the stars
And remember myself in transformation bars
That crept on in through darkness is birthed
The blossoming of the lotus in mirth
To reach towards the light in struggle did find
The enlightenment of a sovereign heart mind

And return to innocence what was created in smoke
To rise now towards Source and connected to stoke
All things in love that bow to the name
In darkness abates the things that are unseen
And transmute the spirit that reveals the means
Of the material world through existence seems.

The Cycles Keep

The cycles keep
The mystery of
The twin flame union
In heirogamic love
On a plane
Where the two are one
And sought the reverence
On this plane to become

The tantric union
In a sacred flame
Was the original concept
Before the magic planes

Before Sofia created from smoke
To understand Source and copulate woke
The sex magic practices of ancient times
That are reveranced by the Illuminate in orgasmic trines

This rare find in this cycle
Was to bring back the original plan
To unite the two as one in brand
Before the Eiyani were divided in half
And the women taken in masculine wrath
To subvert the divine and break the cord
And scatter the power for patriarchal control.

The rising of the feminine is like
The phoenix who births itself from the fire
And spreads her wings from the molton ash
To birth a renewal of templates past
And show with life amidst the crash
How the Dakini rises in this moment meshed.

Through the Looking Glass

Through the looking glass peers
A flipped form of reality
What is real in years
Finds itself upside down in flattery

What is ruling in realms
Is not present here
And remains the controls of society
Behind the curtain peers

The grasping of power like hungry ghosts
Whom can never eat enough
Consumed the consciousness of realities
In things that matter most

We must look beyond the veils of perception
To know the projection reels upside down in streams
And bring heaven on earth in dreams

Know thyself before
The coming of this seed
And realize this reality
Is only a perceived dream

Turn the light around
To find your way down
The illusive world in rounds
That peer through the glass

Know your power to
Alchemize in you
The song that swept you through
The world of what you do.

Be the light within
To manifest your wind
And dawn the day of friends
To find the peace within

Own the sovereignty of
Your sacred heart of love
The releasing of the dove
From your years above

Anchor the light within
For this moment it finds its mend
To let the earth ascend
As we travel with it

Know the place in time
Sets in cosmic clock signs
And melds into andromeda.
Plasma fields that spread
Mark the activation of
DNA light read
Into the dimensions spread
Higher in the octave
Vibrating in the sound
The light body spoken
A new form of rounds

And so it is with ascension
The active play of redemption
From lower reflections given
Through the looking glass.

Third Eye Sight

Will you see me when I AM embodied?
Will you know me when I AM here?
Will you welcome me home for the spirit sullied
The physical form when I draw near?
Do you understand the impermanence
Of my incarnation?
Do you see the mission of importance
To transform the nation?
Do you listen to the ancestors
Who prayed for my manifestation?
And once here to dream this reality
Do you welcome my creation.

Do you see me with third eye sight?
Do you work with me in your might?
Do you balance the universe combined?
In what you call to mind?

Do you control your magical powers?
Do you reap control over the hours?
Do you wait to unfold what sours
The sovereignty of fallen towers.

The gateway is coming in its presence
The time vectors mark existence
And still what is unseen persistence
In all in what drives resistance.

To mark a new age in coming
And still the time is yearning
To birth what is becoming
In realize all what is learning.

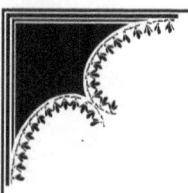

From controlled to freedom.
From prison planet to its kingdom
From slave matrix to liberation
And all who escape martyrdom.

Do you look for the controls?
And perpetuate the projection
While not realizing your co-creation
In what you serve in rejection?

Do you realize the narrative mind?
In what you come to find?
That in all the focus trines
What you don't like shines?

Rather call to mind
The chatter in your brain
To create the heart space binds
The results that are maimed.

Remember your creator spirit
And work that with your heart
To anchor the kingdom of god
In the land that is frought

This is our time to shine
To break the chains of the mind
To cometh forward and find
We are that which is the I AM
Create the world of heart
And remember who you are.

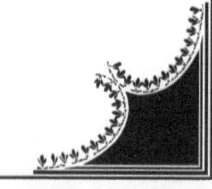

~ Nicole Caswell-Kerrigan ~

The Hunt of the Unicorn

Pure intent is love in action
And is the balance of the reaction
Of the Law of One
From Source sung
The golden rule of sanction.
The purity of the unicorn embodied
Represents a line of Christ like love
A line of David embodiment
Of Buddha mind and truth sent
A purity of heart and soul to run
Sent to attract the maiden be
And so abide for all to see
A marriage of union in peace to become
But those who sought to kill the steed
Tried to empty the purity
In hunting parties to partake of thee
The sow chaos and enmity
The divide from love and fear
To control the masses that came near
Their own actions show the state of affairs
In mind and heart that catch the air
They know not love that cometh near
And so they attack the unicorn in fear
And break the universal law of one
The love that came to embody the sun
They do not know the magic that lies
Within the death and rebirth sighs
And the resurrection is given it ties
The Laws of Maat and heart feather lies
It cannot destroy the love that is
Even though the battle here presents
We are the seed that in darkness grows
And seeds the growth for which we sowed
Know thyself in love and be
The purity of heart that sets you free.

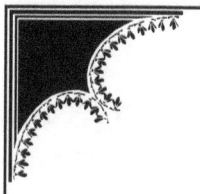

The Emerald Covenant

Respecting the boundaries of the heart activated path
Protects the emerald city access from the grapes of wrath
The golden rule that marks the middle way
To avoid the leaning of duality play
Is known by principal in come what may

The karma dharma wheel in the balance of time
Reveals the actions in integrity rhymes
Its shield to those with a pure heart
And lends to justice when justice is wrought

If broken by intent to cause harm in control
Sets the wheels spinning in action to roll
And responsibility shifts from what energy bounds
To reel that for which we support the rounds.

Please take heed and listen with heart
The emerald covenant guards against thought
It's more than the mind, it's the center of thine
It's the combining of powers of the auric field mine.

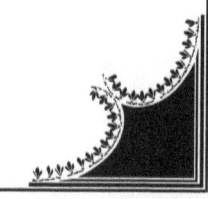

The torris field in energy lines
That form the eternal life lotus trines
Be love and that which you came
Speak your truth in integrity tames
The lies that shroud in wild bazaar
To be the truth you seek that you are

If that which is light shines in the dark
To reveal the revelation of veils which is sought
To rend the curtains that shrouded the veil
To see the controllers that market the hail
And know the projections that lie in the times
Of Plato's Cave and renders the lies

We must stand in our own heart shine
The emerald covenant of shining your light.

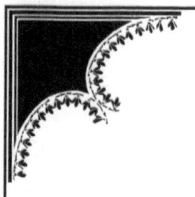
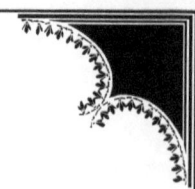

Transcendental Meditation

The ancient action of pushing past the gateless gates of the mind.
To connect with the Divine and to unite humankind.
The Buddhas and the Bodisvittas from the wisdom of the ages
The avatar of the earth though our muses and our mages.
The incarnation of our being with our third eye to understand our seeing.

For acceptance and compassion to help rise above
The suffering and injustice and to forgive in love.
Until we realize our nature. The apotheosis of our minds.
Like a moth to a flame, to know Oneness we are the same.

Like a phoenix in the fire, we develop we grow.
We undress our desire, we start over and reach for something higher.
And in this I do know
That our Chakra crown will glow
It's rays like the corona of the sun
And so it is we are adorned and in this beauty we run.
And so we reflect the Universe we become
A mirror for all to see.

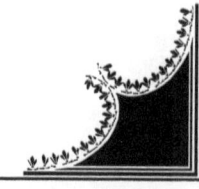

Crystalline DNA

The crystal skulls
From long ago
The age of Atlantis
Tell tales you know
Within the quartz
A program found
Of DNA transformation
From resonate sound
The 13 together
A hidden number
Shrouded in time
And set asunder
Were left behind
To tell the time
When mankind
Would return to blunder
The skull of doom
Some thought evil life
When death would ride
His course in time
Would call out then
And call it back
A star gate portal
Of age reset
What happened then
When Atlantis fell
And the 13 families
Left a tale to tell
We meet again
In spirals of time
To know the resonance

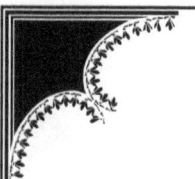

Deeper this time
And hidden within
The crystalline structure
The DNA of those left asunder
Would resonate a vibration now
To share the tale of those who fell
So those who came again with time
Would not repeat the same mind
The technologies that caused the ruin
The sinking of the Kali Yuga
And this spiral would ascend on up
The golden portal to find its way out.
It must be so when uncovering truths
Of all who learn the spiritual paths
Take time to understand the runes
And avoid the evils of the wrath.

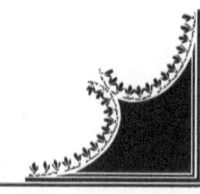

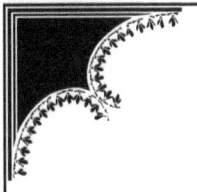

Eyes of a Child

With eyes of a child
I see the void
The darkness and veil
That lies uncurled
The cherubim moves
With chariots of fire
And scrys through the valley
That hides the liar
When false light appears
And intention is sought
For selfish reasons
To imbalance what's wrought
All that shines isn't a golden heart
I uncover the side of the coin that lies
Hidden from the prying eyes
As things fall away once the third eye sees
Another is gained from the pruned root of trees
And what once was hidden in darkness diseased
Is returned to the light to grow with ease.
It transcends through obstacles once perceived
And recreated to embody the mystery.
To realign the ancient and sacred ways
And preserve the integrity of the mystery school days
By looking closely I align what is mine
And return the records to the true timeline.

Who Do You Think I Am?

Am I like this community guitar,
Hung on the wall for all to see,
With an open invitation that says, "play me"?

Who do you think I am?

That I should wish for this?
A friendly embrace that lingers too long,
Or the invitation of a stranger's kiss?

Do you think that I am a lost soul
Roaming from haunted corner doors?
Do you think my love is rivaled
Like all the other lonely souls
Looking for desperation
In a bottomless glass of wine?

Who do you think I am
That my light should seek to find?
The homeless cries in a tired mind.

Who do you think I am?

In this room of smoke filled mirrors I find.

Who do you think I am?
Where this I am presence resides?

— Nicole Caswell-Kerrigan —

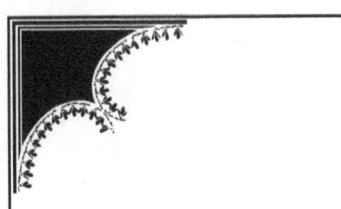
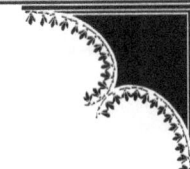

I am my own woman
My own light,
My own strength,
I acknowledge my own fight!
So who do you think I am?

A thing to spite?
A thing to fight?
A thing to play a game?
A thing to hang?
A thing to bring?
A thing to sing of my fame?

Who do you think I am?

A witch to fly?
A bitch to buy?
A fling, a bird?
A quiet fuck?
A thing to suck?

Who do you think I am?

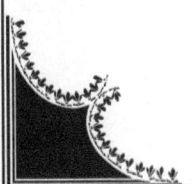

The Voyage of the Dawn Treader

The voyage of the Dawn Treader in chasing the sun
The light that shed that causes to become
Was a journey of darkness taken by some

Claims were made that were not true to Source
And through the perception that valued the course
Stood in truth to abate the state
Of whether or not a bloodline to make
We're vampiric or not to make the name
Seem something it sought to usurp the game
All were created and some fell indeed
To allow the separation to succeed

But the reputation to create the need
To secret of the universe so pray tell
Is the 3-6-9 Tesla said so well
The three sets of three that make the name
To create the universe for all who came
Was three sets of sounds and three sets of light
Created with colors by three guardian rights
The three are one the divine triad made
The fluer de le from the Merovingian came
To show the symbol in throughout
A lucky thirteen in time was route

To be usurped by Anunaki lines
To create the 12 from timelines
They forgot the calander that ran 13
And the tribe of Dan to be unseen
They masked the divine feminine and used her power
To create the Eiyani massacre flower

~ Nicole Caswell-Kerrigan ~

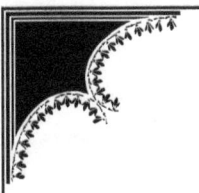
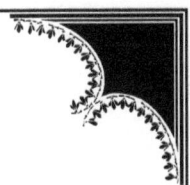

They fought two brothers through realms of time
That caused rifts in quantum space timelines
And created falls in empires of old
Atlantis, Lumeria and Mayan unfold.

To create wealth they created a class
Of slaves that mined the gold to last
For the atmosphere of Nibiru's past
And genetic lines were experimented too
To do the work they weren't willing to do
The misnomer for micro and macro grew

Until the end, until the line
Brought forth Source in end of times
To stop the wars and alien wares
And create the ascention for earth to fare
Just through the gates of the Amenti sphere
To transmute what was created there
From red to green to open the veil
And stop the soul net with the tribal shield

With the eternal life lotus created there
The karmic cycles end in time.
This is the final call
Come back to Source one and all
Be at peace with no more fall
Hear my prayer on the wailing wall.

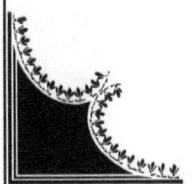

Money Magic Systems

The black magic money systems
From Babylonian times
Creates a fiat of currency
As energy flies
Taking the bull by its horns
As seen in the stock
To create the maritime
Ocean lock

In history creates the image
Of the golden calf lineages.
Were infiltrated with sacrifice
In molton fire resides
Return to the homage
Of the wholeness in time.
Where the cow was venerated
And respected in culture
For its kindness and grace
And it's spirit was ruptured
To be controlled in archaic infrastructures

When time wars were won in Orion's Stargate
And the cyclical loops were cut to abate
And begin to crumble as we move past
The New World Order not meant to last
And into the earth as heaven resides
To witness it with these ancient eyes.

Gateway

On the precipice of the gate
The colossal obstacle that awaits
Before my dreams abates
What transpired of late

I wonder as I walk
The journey of my soul
Was it warrior enough
To take on its goal?

I observe so much pass
That came to me through time
Revealed itself as false
When held up in the light

I detach from the mask
And ponder as I do
Shall this vessel pass
And its temple too?

It's death/rebirth in cycles
Phoenix flame does lie
Breath of fire trials
Ignite the ancestral ties

As all is laid asunder
Has chaos made its plunder
Or peace of god does judge
The breathing in and thunder

Hear the soul has taken
A vessel for the making
And all that is forsaken
Is judged upon the altar

Here with hearts on hire
The chariot of fire
The cherubim of Lyra
The turn of tide for quagmire.

Star of David

From the house of David
A star was born
To examine the tribes
Of the 12 horns
A hidden number
Tied to times of old
That which fell asunder
From legend scorned.
In a jubilee year
And bloodline sent
To tear the veil that was rend.

The revelation that started from Lumeria's past
When templates were taken to the written mass
And distortions created a prison dome
To recycle the souls of the forlorn
Forgetting the lifetimes in cycles sought
The light that came for all who brought

Tumult in seas of men like waves
And set the sun of man in days
The solar flash that comes in rays
That light template of DNA
And connects the conscious and subconscious mind

The plasma bursts in Shumann rays find
The OM set in that hums the heart
And widens the field of auric energy brought
A portal through the great central suns
And central creation to end times run
The hidden acts of Lucifer raise

The light that hides in darkness gave
In three strikes of trishula saves
The severance of ego in control games
We take the matrix in structures sought
To reengineer what heaven's sought
To create a dream of love that brought
A life once here that was once forgot

To return the ways from templates made
Before the distortions had even gave.
A reflection of heaven on earthly days
And so it is and so it saves.

A Genuine Heart

A genuine heart is rare indeed
A sincerity in quest to find a lead
For those embroiled in the speed
Of polarity wars to feed the need
Sociopathic tendencies that create
A problem to now mitigate

In controlled opposition to guard a gate
And spun the fight to litigate.
The middle way and heart path rose
The find the balance and bring the pose
Into the light to walk the way
From obstacles that play what may.

Centering the peace within
Walking away from that which spins
The storm that makes a hurricane watch
To be the eye in the wind to march
Through the drama that spins outside
To find the peace that resides.
Pulling apart the lies from truth
So all that resides is what is pure
I call myself in rest to be
The calmness of the turbulent sea.

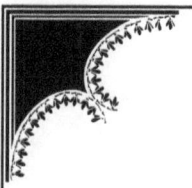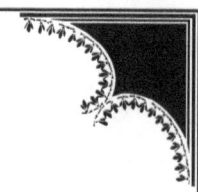

To Save Face

When you spite your nose to save your face
And your pride takes fall to replace
The lion that sat on the Phynx stargate
And carved into a pharaoh face
Belonged to infiltrations to take
To rule Egypt from Atlantean times
The dark magic practices in rules of rhyme
The vrill of the black eye club
A parasitic alien rubbed
Into the third eye and serpent line
To be shown on the forehead in time
Took over the Lyran guardian bloodline
When the stargate of Amentena fell
And caused the Big Bang we know so well

So those who came in with the sun
Saw it set before the day had begun
Napoleon knew the Akashic times
And spewed a cannon ball of crimes
To blast the nose when try to save face
A kind of graffiti from the Merovingian take
When empires grew he knew so well
We're bought by the Lewis and Clark expedition tell
Everything west of the Mississippi fell
Became the United States we know so well

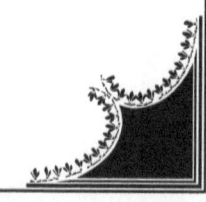

So the 13 colonies were made to grow
And over time corporations know
That each state is run as a different show
And so there is no United I know
Because every law is separated by state
And this the corporations create their fate
To take a rule over the people shall tell
To usurp the sovereignty of those who ascend
From political powers they create a bend

And yet since our ascention line
Came through the gates of the du'at to find
We are playing out our final timeline.

So choose it wisely, choose it well
The ascension gates opened to all who fell
Look past the veil we know so well
When the Phynx began to shut its eyes
The pharaohs fell from quantum timelines
To again allow the sun to rise
The great solar flash through Amenenta cries.

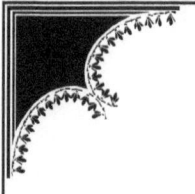

Color Wheel

As the color wheel spins and tones are turned
One to be orange by the fire is burned
One to be cool by the bluish light
Reflects a color despised in sight.
Is just a reflection of perspective you see.
The tones are the colors depicted in me.

Of Syrian nature where blue light was held.
A color not cool but the hottest to meld
A transformation of temperature in alchemical scores
That burns in the brightest and hidden in lore.
I know the wheel and kelvin met
To reflect a harmony of warmth is felt
The indigo race that was held
To transform the inversions and powers that be
Turn the wheel of alchemy
In the ring of fire for all to see

And orange used to reveal a warmth
Of a candlelight glow and intimacy sought.
Color is a reflection of who we are.
There is no separation of that which came
I dispel the nature of the color claim.
And combine all from fractalized light

Into the primal template of principal white.
When I see the colors combined as one
I see the reflection of the sun
And so all is one.

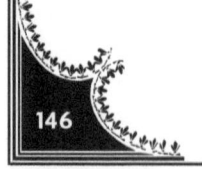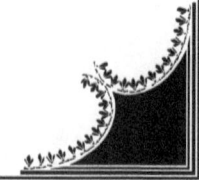

~ Nicole Caswell-Kerrigan ~

Maritime Gateways

Passageways exist by land and by sea
That drives the water in ebb and flow
Listen to the spirit reveal the way
With clairvoyant sight for all to be
The sails unfurl in the suspension bridge
That creates a passage to the other side
And sentinel trees that witness begins
To tell the tale where magic resides
There is a splitting in the turn of tide
Reveal the sands that bide their time

And passages that hover when then on high
To wave over marshlands by bird isle
I see it all as I circle the path
And bike along the boardwalk planks
The reversals on duality struck
The critical mass that makes the plays
And fractured in both light and dark
They establish their checkerboard games

Little do they understand the laws
Of middle path that makes the day
The law of one is truly lost
In the concepts of duality play

And so with transmutation and love
I call upon the Violet flame
I shower the fractions that lost their way
In trusule strikings of ego play
So many have gone astray
To gather power in selfish ways
They forgot the love and law of one
In order to make a name

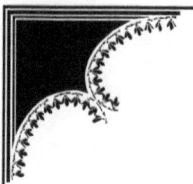

As the grandmother trees witness on land
I give it back with loving hands
And return to source all those thought grand
That lived in mind and no heart concept gave
The source of all that created the ways

A book of life then forged a way
And written carefully by ones own heart
Tipped the balance and they depart
As I seek out those with insight for all
I see fractions within fractions for the call

And those I know I can count on one hand
That practice love unconditionally grand
Is more valuable than all the sands
Of time within the eternity lies
Like diamonds hidden they know the times
Connect with grids to create again
The law of one where duality ends.

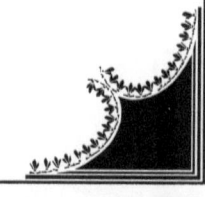

— Nicole Caswell-Kerrigan —

Flame Holder

I hold the light in torch was cast
The eternal flame of source code last
The ancestral ways in prayers of past
And in pillars that raised the mast

I hold the space of matter placed
Between the stars that cast their place
The living waters of light do face
The creation codes that make their way

Within the universe of my soul
The ever-swirling vortex goal
For peace of Source Creator goes
The balance in this play of role

I hold the heart sacred and true
And cast the spark to renew
As the separation grew
The return to innocence who knew
I hold the triad the law of one
The three into the blazing sun
And so it is and has begun
The days of light my beloved sun.

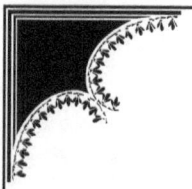
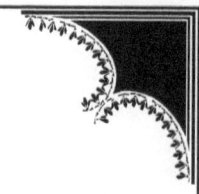

Shakti's Garden

Shakti's garden and guarded gate
By the crystalline platform wait
And all who enter to heal is known
Their intention as the winds have blown
The secrets of the heart is found
In action for those who envy the crown
And if discovered inversions sent
Because the golden rule was wrent

The locks will change and heavenbound
Will hear the cry in silence found
The trisule struck and blade will fall
The decree was sent by heaven's call
And those who entered will know their fall

When peace is given but not respected
When gifts were made to be subjected
And misuse of power I call protection
I know the heart when on inspection

I see with insight and do judge true
The envy that hides inside of you
And measures taken to steal are found
I call out on a cry of sound
And know that there is no where found
Where soul can hide I know the round
And so by source and innocence hides
I return to all that laid the lies.

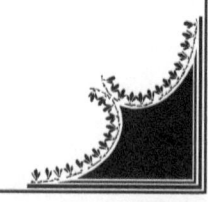

∽ Nicole Caswell-Kerrigan ∽

Xcalibur

I call forth Xcalibur
From the crystal river host
Towards the Stargate of Avalon
And stone of destiny to toast

I call on my Huna name, Haniura
And bring it forth to Camelot by the divine feminine MA.
I call forth the waters
And stir upon the wave
Restore the works of Stonehenge
In which the magi grail lines came.

The sovereignty of England
In silent winds does blow
And finds the sands of time calling
Through the drifting winter snows

I see the castle coming
Through the veil of fog it finds
The unity consciousness humming
As it steps through timelines.

I see the triad
As the three are one
And brings the bifurcation
On the flashes of the sun.

I see the ascending timeline
And anchor the spaces there
Through the Amenti stargate
And the transmutation sphere.

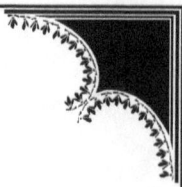

I see the eternal life lotus
Beating with the drum of heart
And returned to strengthen the apperendus
Reversing the distortions from the start

I see the braided threefold cord
That holds our earths in tact
And the grids of each planet
As it layers in the fact
Engineering the planet as it comes into 5D
And settling the scores of heaven so it becomes the peace it needs to see.

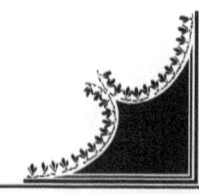

Go Further

"Go further!" you should of heard her say;
"Go further and tell me what you find along the way."
The journey of a thousand miles begins with a single step
So take your leap of faith through the gateless gate and always do your best

Many trials you will find
Will have to be worked out within your mind
But, go further I heard her say

And losses too, will find you
There are sacrifices you must pay
Do not allow fear to deter what you do
"Go further!" I heard her say

For wisdom gained is wisdom earned
You'll learn it by the day
It will transform the essence of who you are
But go further all the same

One day amidst the massive quaking
You will have found that you have awakened
And the obstacles that once felt so tall
Will seem to have grown so small

Necessity will have won the fight
Of all that has come to light
"Go further!" I heard her say

Stonehenge

Stonehenge guards
The portal stands
Kristic spirals in vortex bends

Sentinel boulders in stalwart watch
A restoring of the round table march

Report to structure
That which brought
On silent calls
Where druids walked

And magi holders
Kept what sought
The mystery schools
The ancients taught

Restore the stones
That hold the line
In 1D forms
The sigils find
On faded crowns

And light language codes
Before the time
When language roamed
Kept the stargate once in tact
Became the Albion gateway racked

Into the fluid lines of Gaul
The liquid magic of Avalon calls
Into the circle one and all
By time abided heaven's call
Stonehenge stands for one for all.

∽ Nicole Caswell-Kerrigan ∽

Archon End

The archon rulers
That control the world
Through false time matrices
And constructs unfurl
Indoctrination dictates
Magistrates whirl
Through Ascension timelines
And conversations twirl
Thinking that the patriarchal lines
Is the only way
For an intermitenary to find a way
And sacrifice the heart of crucifixion play
And to question it is twisting and attacking what may
No conversation of peace can than be made

I let go of the conception of the block that is passed
To tear the unity for power to grasp
I spit the thought out of my god sovereign mind
To a god wanting power to calculate the cost
By claiming all power when liberation is lost

There are many that wish to take over the mind
And claim the way beware you'll find
Yeshua said many will come in his name
And claim to be that while false prophets play

It takes discernment to know the way
Unity consciousness is not exclusive
To light a way is not illusive
The work we do to shed the light
And stay in the moment despite the fight
To manifest freedom and do what's right
Is taken in action and integrity find

We take back our power when we don't give it away
For those to take it over in a power play

The Fellowship of the Ring

A soul tribe created and set before time
To incarnate in these avatars along the ley lines
A fellowship of trust and that of deep love
To altar the matter in this matrix above

For all that came which was separate and fallen
And created a distortion for all those who called in
To return the structure to innocence we came
And to help those who floundered inside the game

We came to create balance, above so below
So that heaven wasn't severed from what made it so

Reverse engineered, constructed the planets abound
Brought in the rays and the light of sound
Connect that which needed to be attached back to source
According to the sentience and what practiced remorse

We took our fleet of ships from the sun to bring in
More support to hold the earthly treasures within
To protect the codes of the ancient ones
The fire letters bore that which comes

And worked remotely for third eye sight
To assist the gates to open and let
The stargate controls for which they set

Marked carefully the acts of heart
And witnessed those we loved dearly depart
To relay the balance of the Law of One

And create the peace to blossom begun
We navigated through with all that we got
And assisted each other with the talents we brought

We supported each other the best that we could
To bring in the value of numbers we would
Dissipate systems that kept us as slaves
And communicated in so many ways
Our treasures we had to gleam in the sun
We're given out in the name of love
And gently we bore all given in time
For light codes to anchor, react and refine

Protect that love in balance of self
Had to speak truths when it was brought on the shelf
Integrity and divinity from the highest form
The fellowship of the rings were then born.

Different Attitudes & Viewpoints

Nothing in life can appear more solemn
Than the sharpness of bitter steel
Or cold glass pressed and reflected against a face.
The asphalt sea of crowded apartments and highways
Backroads and bridges
Gleaming spots of light in the lost road of technology

Through it all reaches a blade of grass
Wilted by the pollution of midnight black chimneys
One strand of color, one difference in the world.
Around it can be likened to a true friend.
One best friend, it stands there without the
Heartless feelings of others

Standing alone from its grey surrounding
Like a precious stone hidden in grains of sand

Relationships can be likened to that blade of grass
When it begins to grow for a person
Only in vain it realizes what love is and was
Then that blade of grass breaks like a heart
By the very person who made it grow
Life may not be as simple or as solemn
As the things that exist around us
But isn't it true that through life
We learn living by the little things?

Isn't it interesting how we glean deep truths
From observing the world around us
In order to see ourselves from within?

The Dawn of Pearl Harbor

Over the horizon, the sunrise appears
And the hum of silence whispers what come in years
The wind rolls over the island from old
The lands of MU's secrets of spirals untold

Here comes the planes rapture
They cover on high
The Kamikaze pirates that drive the skies
The battles them muster
Over the maritime flows
And ships then cluster on Pearl Harbor boughs
Waves of men crash and level the shores
And waves of bodies mash into the tales of lore

Replay the horizon from Lumeria's past
The sun rises shine high upon the masts
The cries of those shatter
Through sacrifice gave
Created a reset of times thereafter
To freedoms save
To control the game play

Know the Akashic records that witness the bays
Peace must come thereafter to stop what may

Days in battle are prisons for men
The sun sets over the horizon
The light then sent
A means to stop battles
In final times take
No replays of tattered
Memories to take

Heal the land and souls on high
Create peace in time matter
And love on heaven's sigh.

~ Nicole Caswell-Kerrigan ~

Golden Rays

The doves awake
In golden rays
And perch on high

The grotto maze
Ascending with sighs
Into the skies

The centurion oaks
That line the way
And bamboo whispers
The secrets slips
With the wind
A gentle rustle
To begin again

The water ripples
On a peaceful touch
And sends a healing
Into the thrush
A place to rest
And restore the mind

The owls roost
And light divine
Amidst the green
And serene
Garden rooms
Of pristine

Nature is where I bind my time
As I sit here with the love of mine.

Love Phi

Love phi encircles
At 3.14
A radius encompass
The round of lore
A ratio created
In spherical cells
The golden light creates
The radius of wells

A connection a reflection
A remembrance of times
A cellular memory
In microcosm winds
Fires the cells that emanate
A flowering unfolds
In the stargate

Opens the passage
When love circles phi
And encapsulates plasma
Within the sky.

Source code creation
The tri vecca calls
The three are one
Through the plasma balls
And so above and below is sent
The heaven on earth
The skies are wrent.
A star is born.

Atlantis Loop

Atlantis plundered and now it plays
Within the sands of time it stays
In the shores of American ways
With each obelisks that crosses the lines
And marks the daisy of death energy mines
From the massacre of masculine ties
And plays again in this record of times
Set from England to colonize
To find corporate profits terraform and rise
The clash of cultures turn the tide

Tartaria came and fell
Because of an alien agenda wield
To cash in on controls of real estate
That happened to be earth to contemplate
And have the trade routes assimilate
Their own control that sealed their fate

And so the games play out on earth
From fallen dimensional planes that birthed
Wars above so below were led
And histories hidden from the slave matrix fed
Since they were separate of Source
And made suffering abound that chartered the course

And so we are in the final act
The end of times begin to frack
The rift in space; see the crack
All is playing and coming back
Over billions of years of plays are stacked

And now there is a final call
To come back to Source Creation calls
And so it all befalls. No more spiraling cycle balls

Connect to source or return to dust
The second death begins to rust
The siphoning of energy all that must
Since it all exist at critical mass
It must show the ways that erred the past
And set the transmutation cast

To end the wars when separation made
A house of cards a spade a spade
Come the fall it has shown the day
And no more time has given way.

Merchant Ships

The merchant ships are shattered
Their tears create the sea
Of implements that followed
In events not meant to be

A crystal pyramid requested
Was sent along the line
And created a security measure
The package lost along in time
But Jupiter gazes met
And the shipment was secured
So the implements to reinstate
Did not need to be recurred

I took responsibility
To pay for what was received
And dropped the charges implemented
That was lost along the seas

A false accusation had arisen
From public information imposed
A blockage was created
As the golden gates were closed

Upon the merchant man who scattered
And tried to create the blows

The transmutation sat
Inside the purple box
That sang with a pitch so high
To transform the imposed cost

With zero point affirmations
The pyramid began to sing
To open the zero point measures
And create an auric ring

I heard the sound a calling
Source Creation codes on hire
Met with the solar flares a balling
On the elements of fire

The light and sound created
A quantum jump timeline
And set the rhythm of the universe
Back to Source Code to find

The Fallen Flower of Life

Down falls the obelisk
The fallen phallic symbol
To create a flower of life
As sacred geometry nimbles

The inverted structure shaken
By the sphere down below
That contains adamantine particles
In a counterclockwise flow

To return the timelines fallen
Into Source Creation codes
And to alchemize the energy
As time returns the flow

Below the Washington Monument
Energy leys below the lines
And fades into the distance
A return to innocence finds

Because the Akashic records
Reveal a hidden truth
The founding fathers embed
A dark magic that stewed
A corporation, a disunited sect
That took the power of peoples
To create the chattel met
Slavery mindset followed
A battle then was set

And civil war now plays
Within the divided and conquer crept
The fall of a great nation
Because the Law of One withstood
The material creation
Of the brotherhood

And so the incarnation
Appeared within the time
To give back the people power
So read between the lines
When balance is not taken
For control in nature sets
Source Code infiltrated its creation
To allow the bifurcation tests

Starborn Counsel

The Starborn Counsel
In starfire stands
In the petals of the lotus
In Crystalline sands
Of times come together
From lands long ago
Fire the transmutation
From the iron mountain show
Up on the wheel that createsthe wave
The maharic seal of vecca symbols gave
Create the blue lotus with petals unfold
Lays the transport of the light bodies told
Carries the seal up the 3 fold cord
To be placed under the broken soul net floor
And then through the openings from 34 degrees
Northeast to degree sixty three
We enter the net with divine unity
And move the field as we combine as one
Cancel the energies from the soul net run
Transmute the mountain with the sorcerer's stone
Runs the wheel to the North Star roam
Fires the seals to to shield the lines
And create the gold through the mineral trines.
As we meet by the eternal waterfall
The eye that sees and watches all
Where the falcon resides
Of the Paladore halls
Crystal facets found there
Bring heaven to earth
As the miasmas fall
The organic line births
Through the vesica Pisces
In the world of mirth.
The golden ley lines from the eternal lotus rise
And anchors the earth through the lines

Plasma Particles

As above as so below
The plasma particles give way to flow
Through the Schumann
And away they go
In electromagnetic fields they sow
Through the awakening that permeates soul
The prison planet net by row
Weakens the structure as consciousness rises
Beyond the veil and into the miasmas
The golden portal three fold cord
That travels with the Excalibur sword
Brings in the maharic shield
To protect the energies to travel and yield
And through the broken grids they set
The balance of the electric grid
To magnetize the force field set
And cancel the force field net
And then with the portal let
The eternal lotus grid to find
And replace that which binds the tide.
A Kristic grid so above as below
To reflect that in the uni sun glows
And so the geometry may be let in
To establish the organic timeline sent
Is my wish as I patiently wait
And place my prayers upon the gate
Of counsels I beset my fate
And once the call is to be had
The iron mountain transmute to gold
Through ancient alchemy untold
Connects the sections of heart base mind
To find the zero point karma/dharma wheel grind
And anchor in the Kristic timeline.

— Nicole Caswell-Kerrigan —

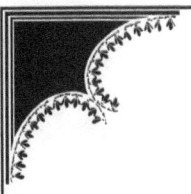

The Nibirian Grid

The Nibirian diodic crystal grid
Made of selenite swords
We're placed under Stonehenge
From the fallen angelic wars.
Many who came before me
Like Yeshua 12 and more
Came in with DNA templates
To break down the door.
Where unable to stop the grid
Before ascension came
So another round of coming
Would happen in the game.
Long after Camelot
And now into this day
The golden ark of covenants
Was deeply hidden away.
Where no one thinks to look
And so it began the play.
The rod and staff within me
The plasma in my blood
I came in to transmute powers
And reversals run
Through Jehovian Annunaki templates
And broken contracts made
Are now over in time through
Source presence plays
A return to innocence
And metatronic ways
Reversing fire letters
That caused suffering
Effects the speech of people
And division brings
And so the experiment is ending
With the magi grail line kings.

The Palace of Alhambra

The palace of Albumbra
Was changed in spelling tactics
And many historical records
In ages long ago
Before the times unfurled
Of what we began to know
Existed a fountain in the garden
It's flow came from the lotus born
And waterways intertwined
Through the portal realms of time
The reflection pool contains
A secret hidden in the lines
That shows the way of northern points inside
The latticework windows inlaid
Allows light to show its work
Lays ways to maze like gardens
And waterways unfurl
And cedar craftsman inlaid
Inthe ceilings up above
Reflect the heavenly realms
In the dimensions up above
The history through records
Began to call my name
And with Ashakic records
Unfurled in the game
Return to me through tears
In waterways make its flow
A reflected building built
Of the heavens I wish to show.

Interlay

Intersecting realities
Exist in multidimensional times
In quantum aspect lines
One is yours
And one is mine.
Just because I remember
Creating stars in the sky
Doesn't mean stars are A.I.
Doesn't mean they don't exist
From an organic timelines where my reality lives
From stargates that open and connect the two
Live parallel timelines between my reality and yours.
Just because one reality is taught
Does not mean that I consent
To having artificial intelligence.
Doesn't mean that my soul came to accept
The way a World Order presents itself
Or has tried to establish a reset.
I came to liberate and bring an end
To all those who would like to enslave
The humans in this matrix game.
I do not consent to controls
And find my way out of black holes
Reverse the polarized concepts
Into unity consciousness
Bring the black and white together as one
As peace is returned to heart
It is my place to impart
My reality in conceptual timelines.

Letting Go

I am letting go with gratitude
Those who offered platitudes
And set themselves to usurp
Powers not meant to be
I am living with the latitude
To allow the vertical solitude
Of ascension in my play
So I can see the balance
And the return to innocence give way

I know who I AM
The perceptions that recalled
The multitude of manipulations
That created a free fall.
I explained my station
It was seen there on high
But continued with manipulation
And with this I say goodbye.
I am tired of explaining
That if higher self is sent
Than a silent retreat can be empowering
Instead of feeling wrent
I am tired of accusations
That reveal a low vibration
It is the revelation for
Love that seeks a balance
And tries to create a talent
In the best that I could offer
Was continuously cut down
With words that were sharp as swords
And brought be to the ground

There was no accounting
Of actions that hurt
And I don't wish to return
The vibration that gave alert
So I walk away with love
Because it could not stand its place
And spirit now recalls
The actions of two faced
Illumination separated
One words don't balance well
And so the scales are shifted when the archetype
Sent spells.

I've graduated from MK Ultra
This is my final show
And my severance I plunder
As fertilizer for growth.

False Profits

False profits abound
When currency is passed
For an ability to speak
In exchanges crash
A fiat system of hoarding gold
The Montauk Programs
Of mind control horns
Scalar technology
Minds cast and bred
To create false realities
And false concepts led
Weighted with iron
Shackled and bred
False profits abound
When they dream in bed

I AM the voice
That is calling from old
The ancient ones scatter
Of gnostics untold.
Of silence whispers
That carry on wind
And create the storm
That carries and sends
The false profits scatter
The vibration cannot hold
The truth that lies in matter
To this matrix rolled

I AM coming with resonance
To return those who bore
Censoring the feminine
To hear her roar!

For those who cannot tolerate
Truth comes in peace
My peace then returns
And the innocence cease

I AM the calm
I AM the storm
The choice is your heart
And your severance is scorned

The Kristic Spiral

We have come to have undone
The spirals of ruin
The run reversals of time
To those that imbue them
In counterclockwise motion
The Kristic spiral unties
The spells that cast to cue them
In light codes unwrey.
Reset the ley lines
And grid patterns run
Set them in golden
Rays of the sun
So above as below
The matter is set
To ways it bestows
And encase to unlet.
Connecting the markers
To points they do bet
And unravel the stalkers
For duality met.
The guardians of counsels
And covens have let
To fly with white dragons
With visions have kept.
Within DNA activations
Each one takes the stance
And draws up the plans
To promenade the prance
And with love and intention
The highest timeline set
To create the emancipation
In liberation bets.
The freedom for all
In balance is kept
The planes do recall
Return to innocence incept.

~ Nicole Caswell-Kerrigan ~

The Age of Aquarius

The Age of Aquarius is marked by a Yuga cycle shift
And heralds the great solar flash as we move through the rift
Once the earth meets it place within the cosmic clock
The galactic core vector of the piscian ticks
And lands its hand on the marker rifts
The space time continuum marked by the vesica Pisces ankh
Is the eye of the needle through the bifurcation mark
It starts with Pluto who enters Aquarius first
And through the column of time in the two pillars of
The eleventh month of Novermer
Through the temple mounts struts
It shows the collective the things that must be seen
And rips apart the veils of the government mainstream
Of those who display narcissistic tides
And tear apart the country by not caring for the lines.
The Antichrist in matter for all who work about
And run towards controls to loudly scream and shout
The last hurrah of power like military fists do bind
All they can shower to prevent sovereign time.
Until the day dies gather, three strikes and then they go
In a battle for world power but this in peace I know
That within the Keiper Belt, the dwarf planets there reside
Come into existence within consciousness abide.
They await a further calling that is not like the above
And sing with the praise of the light language song
When the solar flash does come its its climax we will see
A new way of manifesting our god free sovereignty
Like Nicola Tesla who wisely once said
The universe is made of frequency, vibration and energy
The light of matter will change our matrix dear
To encompass that of heaven to which we all hold near
So hold the line you light workers
Who incarcerated on this time
And know no weapon will befall you
To the Christ like mind.

Somatic Sound Circle

Fear is a vibration
On a sine wave sound
That anchors in your seat of power
And through the sacral energy met
Is transmitted through the hertz
Of 174 set
And forms a mandala
When cymatics takes a shape
To open the door of possibilities
For an alchemy to make
Another way of seeing
Another form of being
A different way of meeting
The inner self of birthing
The letting go and trusting
The alchemy of change
And with the scope of range
A new experience of
A song of
Light language love.

Tuatha De Rune

The rune of Tuatha
Is a sigil rite
That guards a doorway
To the Viking might
It's Celtic heritage
In Druid lore
Insights the light language
Sign before
Connects a realm to come online
Through Stargate function
Ascention divine
It stands on stones
That float in air
And knows the names
Of those who fare
The Tuatha de danaan
Who keeps the temple
Inside the treasures
Of earthen vessels
The cauldron, spear and sword of light
Is seen on the stone of might
To know the kings that reign on site
A guardian measure and treasure rite.

Peace Treaty

There must a be peace between the dragons and lyrans
To never allow battles to break the law of heaven
The two guardian races
That created and stations
The flow of the Stargates to have begun
The cementing of the Law of One.
There must be a knowing
In the middle way
To create the Emerald Covenant
For the times that must stay
Between the battles and come what may
The treaty of peace
To pillar its strength
There must be a knowing
That Source is glowing
In light all is roaming
In extremes can find
The heart path storming
It's purity forming
In all the ways it it will leave the old behind
I am both Lyran and dragon informed
The ties that lie broken over ways that loomed
Are tied now together within the phynx overhead
And turned into heart green that once beamed red
I see with the heart, its throne given find
To reel in the peace once warred over find
Know the way that's not too frought in mind
With extremes of parydimes that were battled when sought
Know the peace from the balance within
I send this on high to Sophia on wind.

~ Nicole Caswell-Kerrigan ~

Expansion

The effortless expansion in experiencing breath
Can relax the mind and find peace and rest
The shift inside to quiet the mind
From the exhaustion of fears that are left outside
What identity role is attached
To find the defense and reaching at last?
What illusions need to quiet the thoughts
That attach the identify of pain to lots
What are the labels that twist the intention
To reveal the temperance of lasting creation?
What conditions find that limit the mind
To expand in unconditional form to find?
Can we settle in peace to know at least
What balance is made when we rest or feast?
What identity finds silence in choice
To know the love within at most?
If the body inside is well and good
And can pour out loving for others would
The temple of body and service does find
Rest from the pain body mind.
Respect the life in roles that may
Creep up in life and in our play.
A place for a time and a time for a place
A choice to be given in what we face
In mortality in obstacle is also a making
Of transformation of being and taking
Be the still in the eye of the storm
Awaken as the winds are born
Fully knowing that moments do find
The power of now and the stillness of mind.

Boots On The Ground

Boots on the ground
Resonate its sound
And dance all around
In light language love
See from afar
The grand game ajar
And know this so far
Its success at its lore
Envision the dance
See the light prance
In mandala faced happenstance
For co creative stars
A symphony of sound
Resonates its rounds
And spirals all around
To install the form
And build the world of
The song danced with love
As it weaves its music
Through the waters below
And stands with a glow
Of laughter and flow
Of joy and of sower
To seed the Aquarian age
It rolls over land
And mountains so grand
Soothes the desert sands
To create the new runes
And takes the cake

~ Nicole Caswell-Kerrigan ~

For the candles sake
To envoke the wake
Of the waves on high
Speak with a sigh
A trip fallen by
And light the night
With blissful creation
To spark the rainbow nation
And here I am stationed
To create center stage
Move light into waves
And secure conscious creation
To be Source in form
Grounded and stationed.

Life Elixir

The life elixir of medicinal plants
Reap the golden liquid of
The apothecary of nature
To soothe the body song
The apotheosis of this kind
To heal the body soul and mind
The holistic power of
The triad of manifested love
To raise the vibration of
The frequency in Mother Earth
As she births from the land
To alchemize the temple within.

Winged Alchemy

Spiraling into the temple
Of the embodiment of self
Bringing in the light of life and Mother Earth's wealth
To drum with the mystery
If choosing life in alchemy
This sacred space in Shamanic love
Knowing the horizontal plane
And that above
Though the gates of hell are open
And heaven waits on high
I run the path of the middle way
To know both as I pass by
I resonate with the alchemy
To be the transmuter of change
As the violet fire lights the gates
Because they know my name
I rise with the spire
Become one with the fire
And know the realms for hire
To reflect a perfect love.

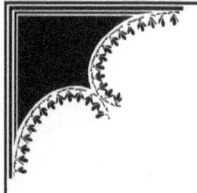
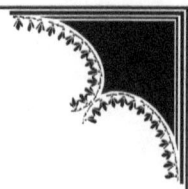

Butterflies

Butterflies transition
And transmute in form
What was once begotten
A new life is born
The chrysalis phase
That encumbers the mass
Allows the old to dissolve
For a birth to task
Marked by wings
The form takes flight
When dried in the sun
And unfurled with the sight
We transform our lives
To become to something new
As butterflies form
It dissolves what is scorned
We contemplate change
And embody the new
To complete transformation
And transmutation grew.

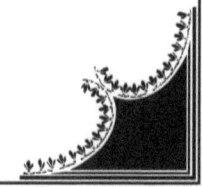

The Elysian Fields

The key code of gods
The unlocking of space
Of pillars and rods
Of Edenic paradise
And royal courts
Held at the edges
Of earths land hedges
A river Styx ran
And came through to the Danube
The odyssey of virtue
The waterways ran through
The golden gate of Shamballa
A peace lies without
To those who held fodder
To drama and shoutout
To those who were humble
And held integrity high
Were held one the courts
Where the music were nigh
A part of heaven on a heavenly plane
Set apart for paradise to know thy name
As lush gardens ran through rivers of gain
Like snaked varmalas in fragrant rain
Temples that stapled the hills alongside
Peaked over mountains and passageways ride
From secrets below and mountains that peaked
We're shrouded in mists as birdsong did keep
And zephyros winds so gentle and true
Whispered through willows as secrets blew
And rocked the fairies that lie in the land
To slumber a sleep of echos so grand
The hum of a lullaby and fragrance did seek
To lull the joys of the humble and meek.

Tataria

The mud flood swept
with frequency fields
And shook the earth
Of energy yields
To bury the system
That once roamed alive
For giants who turned
To stone arrived
Fossilized as mountains
Cliffs abide

-Petrified.

Silent in measure
They sleep below
And through somatic gilphs
The ley lines flow
The star forts created
As above so below
Became prisons to hold
To harvest and sow.

Melted ruins half showing the yield
We're built on towers
-Parasite fields
To take the systems
They build another
To play their music
Of 440 fodder.

~ Nicole Caswell-Kerrigan ~

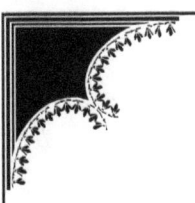 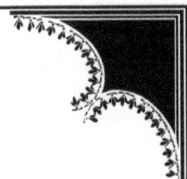

The smart phones and towers
Signal 5G
Hum a radiance of vibration to be
And disconnect organic matter to see
The artificial intelligence grid to see.

Come back to nature
Listen to sound
That heals the body
The mind and ground

Know thy history
Feel thy truth
Empower thyself
Rise in cuth

Resurrect the cities that sleep below
And hum the song the ancients knew
Crystal cities of old that grew
From sacred geometry and spirals knew
The fields that healed
That allowed for growth
To find the anchor that matters most.

 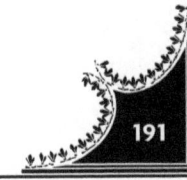

Copy Cats

They mimic and snicker at real world design
And envy the radiance of Source Code divine
They commit to drama and ego is sought
To build something greater for nations to fought
Over energy fields, stargates grew
To seed the parasites through parallel worlds
They brought in AI to lower the sound
And fodder the cities and muddy the ground
They reset through floods and rewrote the books
And hid the true history and bury the goods
They took the rest that was given in worlds
And sealed the gates to fodder the gods
They broke down structures so grand and true
To separate Source in dream time too
The architect manifested through physical planes
And took those yielding to government reigns
Brought in parasites to feed off the crowds
And shattered the truth in silent clouds
They created an order to give power below
Through black magic arts and self service flew
They spliced and diced genetic life
And made hybrids to walk the streets in rife.
They faltered through towers and fed the crowds
Through GMO matter to tarnish the rounds
They created the doctrine for control of mounds
Of what they lie buried beneath the ground.
False light they carry and yield it on high
The inverted Illuminati to trick the sigh
But truth through matter rises nigh
And gold refines as impurities rise.

Nicole Caswell-Kerrigan